MW01223421

faithsongs

faithsongs

ancient psalms for today

MARK ANDERSON

DeNovo Publishing

DeNovo Publishing Inc.
PO Box 347, Lynden, WA 98264
www.denovopublishing.com

© Mark Anderson 2010

All rights reserved. No part of this book may be reproduced in any manner
whatsoever without prior written permission from the publisher, except in
the case of brief quotations embodied in critical articles and reviews.

Pages 287-88 constitute a continuation of the copyright page.

Every effort has been made to trace ownership of copyright materials. In the
event of an inadvertent omission or error, please notify the publisher.

Liability for all statements made in this book belongs exclusively to
DeNovo Publishing Inc.

ISBN 978-0-615-42738-6

Cover design by Rod Sawatsky. Ancient Psalms text image from Dead Sea
Scroll 11QPs (dated ca. 30-50 CE). Model: René Thomas
Printed and bound in the United States of America

For the members of Jacob's Well—
lovers of God, his good earth &
the community around us

For Cathy, my partner-for-life
without whose grace, patience &
faith, it could not have been written

Contents

Disclaimer

This Book May Not Be for You

Mention God, faith or religion to a lot of people nowadays and you find yourself in a veritable minefield of misunderstandings that threaten all useful discussion. Since I'm keen to reduce, not increase that risk, I'd like to start by saying what this book is not.

Be it Christian, Muslim or Jewish, there's a lot of religion strutting around these days that's totally egocentric. And this book is no paean to egofaith.

What do I mean by egofaith? It does the odd good deed—sometimes more—puts money in the plate and knows all the right words to say. But so concerned is it with appearances, keeping up with the Joneses whether materially or "spiritually" and the photogenics of faith, you might think its adherents are all somehow running for office. It talks a fine line about being a good person, pleasing God or even knowing God. And it's often blatantly evangelistic, looking for new recruits who will make their recruiters look even more "spiritual" for having won them.

What these believers don't seem to realize is that everyone sees through their religious devotions. That is, everyone not into the pretense and head games their religion runs on. Egotism isn't that hard to detect if it's truth you're after.

But alas, there's more. Throw into this mix either faith's

commercialization or its crass politicization and you increase its ugliness tenfold. I refer on the one hand to tawdry televangelists and other religious empire-builders who prey on well-meaning, but naïve and softhearted people. You have only to surf to the right channel or take your place in the assembled crowd. If you're into religion, the leader knows his business and his presentation is slick enough, why not give him your generous support?

On the other hand, I refer to people convinced it's their destiny to take political control. Some by telling the "silent majority," moral or otherwise, to listen up and vote or picket as they say. But also by silencing their people's honest questions and objections through manipulation, intimidation and religious doubletalk and typically muzzling their women in the process. Some by fulfilling a grand destiny that somehow puts the remote in their hands, enabling them to fast-forward us to the end of the world and their eternal reward. And some by the free use of physical aggression— anything from lawsuits and spittle to scripture burning and suicide bombs.

Having tragically gone mainstream, egofaith is no more the preserve of fragmented cults and fringe groups. The only good thing about this is the clarity it brings to one basic truth we so often forget. Namely, that when it comes to faith and unbelief, opinion polls don't count for much, one way or another.

How could all this have happened though? How could so many good people have been so misled? Surely they weren't seeking deception when they started out.

On the contrary, they began with the same longing for truth we all have. But we don't exactly start out with a clean slate either. Our parents and our culture as a whole were already messed up long before any of us ever came along.

And this world is no easy place to navigate spiritually. How many mistaken notions of God and of love there are and yet these are spiritual realities second to none. With danger and deception on every hand, it's the Temple of Doom—minus Indiana Jones. Many good people are taken in and sadly become part of the toxicity that threatens to destroy them.

The Psalms Are Different

If you loathe egofaith as I do, you'll be relieved to know this book isn't remotely interested in promoting it. In fact, you won't find a book in the Bible more antagonistic to egofaith than the Psalms. While the psalmists' extreme honesty may be problematic to us at times, there's certainly no denying that it's not the kind of faith that lends itself to smug, self-serving reports or neat and tidy little photo ops.

Egofaith often claims to have a biblical basis, but it skews every Bible verse it touches. So the fact that some brands of egofaith make liberal use of the Psalms in their public worship is highly misleading. The Book of Psalms is open to misuse just like everything else. Being poetry, the psalms are pithy, inspiring and quotable. And the phrasings of ancient poetry are especially easy to misconstrue. Still, no one reading the Psalms carefully and honestly could possibly end up with egofaith.

So if you're willing to consider what honest, open faith might look like, I invite you to discover the Bible's ancient "faithsongs." Being full of truth, they overflow with freedom, blessing, life and joy. I pray all these things will touch you in reading *Faithsongs* as deeply as they've touched me in writing it.

There's no denying that in all its various forms egofaith has become a major alternative to authentic biblical faith. In fact in terms of sheer numbers, it sometimes seems to be edging truth out. But if it's egofaith you're into, read no further. This book is not for you.

Intro

Why Read the Psalms?

Ours is a faith-challenged age. We believe in everything and nothing at once. We know we're spiritual, as much *above* animal *as* animal. But we're deeply conflicted over religion, drawn to its beauty and truth no less than repelled by its shallowness and hypocrisy.

So we strike out on our own. Or just muddle on, ignoring faith except in our darker hours. But either way, we come up short.

Ancient Israel's* Book of Psalms[1] may seem an unlikely place to find help. But the psalms were written to give hope and courage to believers wracked by doubt. And to this day they've lost none of their power. Our only challenge is learning to read them well. If we do that we'll see that they offer us true wholeness in a broken world.

What the Psalms Are About

If you asked me to say what the Psalms are about in ten words

---

*I've included a glossary of terms most of the Psalms' first readers were familiar with (pp. 261-64). I mark each glossary entry's debut in a chapter with an asterisk.

or less, I'd borrow Will D. Campbell's line from another context: "We're all bastards but God loves us anyway."[2] While Campbell's language may be raw, he's got it right. Misbegotten daughters and sons that we are, God welcomes us home in spite of all we have and haven't done. Tells us to come as we are. Wants us to know him and be remade in that knowledge. And he not only cares about us as individuals, but is also committed to the healing of our world.

This will come as a surprise to many in the West, where faith in God has been horribly truncated by many of its promoters. The shallow self-centeredness of their version is as embarrassing as it is hurtful. For years it's made anyone in our secular universities professing faith in God the subject of ridicule and scorn. It's also why the spirituality so many people are open to nowadays isn't biblical and why so many give up their faith in God with no contest, for either the cynicism of the day or the spirituality of the month.

God's Gift to the World

But assuming it's true biblical faith we're discussing, the idea that Yahveh,* God of the ancient Israelites, has anything to do with us today will strike many as bordering on ludicrous.[3] Sometimes I myself have wondered why God didn't just put on a massive sound and light show, followed by a personal appearance, all somehow broadcast live to everyone on the planet in their own language. Would it really convince us though?

According to Psalm 19, he's actually done the sound and light show and its broadcast is continuous. But he's done it without appearing to give the speech and accept our standing ovation. And without that many remain skeptical.[4] They seem to think that if he does exist, he ought to at least show them the courtesy of doing things as *they* see best. But why shouldn't God do things *his* way? What makes us so sure *we* know best?

The Bible has God entrusting his special revelation to a single nation under heaven. And that means revealing himself to them in ways that fit their unique language, culture and thinking. But even so, his intention from the very first was to bless the entire world through them.[5] So we mustn't be overly put off by the nationalist aspect of the Psalms or the Tanakh,* the Hebrew Bible it's a part of.

One reason God chose to work with a single nation is that he's never been remotely interested in having us embrace some mysterious, ethereal, non-communal truth. He's always wanted us to live his truth in very practical, everyday, down-to-earth ways. Things like caring for the earth, being generous to the poor, welcoming the outsider and loving our neighbor as ourself.

So he chose to show one nation and culture how it would look in their particular case. It's undeniably going to look different in other nations, cultures and times. But at least he gave us one clear picture to go by. By reading carefully and listening with all our hearts, we find the Psalms still speak to us today as they did so many centuries ago.

The Challenge of Scripture

As heartening as the universality of God's revelation to Israel is, it brings with it three daunting challenges. The first is cultural. Having to understand a message given to people remote from us in both time and place is a bit like having to read a book wearing someone else's glasses. It requires serious effort and concentration. It may give us the odd headache. And we may get some things wrong even with the best of intentions.

But here we must fall back on the work of the many gifted linguists and biblical scholars who have given their lives to making Israel's ancient scriptures intelligible to us. And we must ask God even as we ask ourselves: If his truth looked so different in this culture and nation, how is it to look in ours?

Some find it unbelievable that God would require such hard thinking of us and make us depend on the work of fallible scholars. Others are offended that God would apparently align himself with an imperfect—for example, male chauvinistic—culture. But loving God was never intended to be a solo enterprise, was always to include our minds and requires far less patience and humility of us than it required of God in the first place.[6]

The second challenge we face is moral. We're naturally repulsed by some of the Tanakh's morals. We find some of its legal prescriptions, its military campaigns, its treatment of women and the psalmists' cursing of their enemies contradictory, even barbaric. And sadly, many of these things have been used to bolster the narrowness and injustice of elites in distinctly different cultures and so given skeptics much to attack.

We can be assured of three things here though. First, some of the objectionable morals have very different import in our culture and time from what they originally had. Second, some of them may demand that we reassess our own culture because we too have skewed things on ourselves. And third, some simply show Yahveh's willingness to work with the imperfect Israelites right where they were, not making the impossible demand that they change everything at once. We may not like this but we can also take great comfort in it because it tells us God won't demand perfection in order to work with us either.

In meeting the moral challenge, we must rely on our best scholars and, equally important, come with hearts that long to understand. Because if we simply seek objections to hide behind, we won't have far to look. Three centuries ago Blaise Pascal wrote, "Truth is so obscure in these times and falsehood so established that unless we love the truth, we cannot know it."[7] If anything, Pascal's words are truer still today.

Many find it unreasonable that God would ask so much and

make his truth so easy to misread, so vulnerable to attack. But what speaks with perfect clarity to one culture invariably distorts things to another. Loving God has always called for a joint allegiance of heart and mind. We must sincerely seek to find.[8]

The third challenge involves truth's dynamic and interactive aspect. Since God's truth isn't just cerebral or formal, we must learn to live it out in the constantly changing circumstances of our lives. Even Moses' law, given in the Torah,* wasn't meant to be an exhaustive casebook covering every conceivable situation that might arise among Israelites. Just like us, the ancient Hebrews had to ask God moment-by-moment how to apply his truth to their individual situations.

Much of the time the correlation was clear and obvious. But often it required far more—heart-searchings in the middle of the night, sacrifices* offered at dawn, prayers and pleadings. This challenge may not strike us as particularly hard. But I suspect more people have abandoned faith in its toils than in the other two combined.

Again, many are stunned to learn that faith requires so much of us—body, mind, emotions, heart, will. But truth has always been addressed to the whole person.[9] Why would God want just *parts* of us when his aim was never to just save our souls, but rather to make us *whole* again?

What the Psalms Are

Written for both public and private worship, the psalms are prayer songs addressed to God. The book compiles 150 of these songs and covers a fairly wide range of genres, everything from the lament—akin to a spiritual or blues piece—to the exuberant song of praise—think Queen's "We Are the Champions," but with God as the One we celebrate.[10]

While the entire book is sometimes attributed to David,

scholars agree that David didn't write all 150 psalms. He was doubtless a major contributor. But the Davidic designation that precedes many psalms was probably added to the text by the book's compiler(s). And while tradition takes it to mean it was written "by David," it can also mean written "for David" or "about David."

Beyond their human authors, the Hebrew community that received these scriptures saw the Psalms as inspired by God,[11] as God's idea of prayer. And that's why the Psalms are such a great place for us to begin. The psalmists are masters in this business of applying truth to life's ever-changing situations. They give us, not mere religious formulas, but rather tried and true models for fellow God-seekers to follow. Because while ritual and form played a vital role in Israelite worship, they were never meant to replace the heart's spontaneous crying out to God.

Another reason to begin with the Psalms is that they're anything but neat and tidy. Sebastian Moore describes them as "rough-hewn from earthy experience."[12] In fact, they're full of raw emotion, not all of which would be considered suitable for polite society today, let alone a religious worship service.

But Eugene Peterson observes that their very messiness helps us correct our thinking about God. We think he'd only want to hear from us when we're on our very best behavior. But the Psalms tell us he's more concerned with our being honest with him than anything else. After all, he knows all our inmost thoughts.

Prayer, says Peterson, isn't "what good people do when they are doing their best…" but rather "the means by which we get everything in our lives out in the open before God." Far from needing special vocabulary or some singsong lilt, prayer is as elemental and personal as each of the psalms.[13]

And whatever else we do with them, let's not overlook the obvious: that the psalms are meant to be prayed. By praying the psalms, we enter into the psalmists' spirituality and are liberated by its freedom, intimacy and ordinary everydayness.[14] By praying them from the heart, we make them truly our own.

Some Whys and Wherefores

Each reading here includes a fresh paraphrase of the psalm, followed by a meditation and a brief prayer. Since I'm neither a Hebrew scholar nor a linguist, I seriously pondered omitting my paraphrases. But paraphrasing the text has been so central to its working the soil of my heart and to the meditation that sprang from it that it seems unthinkable for me to omit them. I encourage you then to read them alongside your most trusted translations, praying simply that God would speak to you through his Word.

Some will wonder why I've chosen to transliterate the Hebrew YHWH or YHVH as Yahveh—pronounced Yah·vay[15]—instead of translating it "LORD" as most English versions do. Simply put, since Yahveh is what all the ancient Hebrew texts say, restoring the name to its actual use in the Psalms gives us a clearer sense of the world it was proclaimed to. This was the name God revealed to Moses as his personal name. So first and foremost, it set the psalmists' God apart from all his rivals in the surrounding nations. Yahveh was the God who had made his covenant with Abraham, Isaac and Jacob and freed his people from slavery in Egypt.[16]

I don't mean to say that Yahveh is the name we must call God by today. Only that we're right to use it in connection with what he says of himself in the Psalms and the rest of the Tanakh.[17] If some readers object to its foreignness, I fully understand. But on the other hand, the psalms are deeply rooted in the history and culture of the ancient Hebrews. Using their name for God helps us keep their context clearly in mind.

With regard to my use of gender-specific pronouns referring to God, I have no doubt about God's encompassing both male and female in himself. But as readers will already have seen, I almost always use male pronouns. I know this is a sensitive issue and I sincerely apologize to anyone who is offended by it. I do it partly out of deference to the biblical story and partly to avoid stylistic awkwardness.

Some may be surprised to see that I've taken a number of the psalmists to be women. Having so long assumed Davidic authorship of the Psalms, many readers have come to see all the psalms as at least written by men.

In fact, there's no lack of evidence for women psalmists. So I suspect women composed a good number of these psalms too. Exodus 15 ascribes the great "Song of the Sea" to Miriam and Moses.[18] It also seems that Deborah composed the psalm celebrating her victory with Barak over Sisera in Judges 5. And Psalms 18 and 113—along with the virgin Mary's Magnificat in the Gospel of Luke[19]—were inspired by Hannah's psalm in 1 Samuel 2:1-10. So there's much to attest to the role of women in leading the Israelites to pour out their hearts to God in psalm.

Admittedly, far fewer women than men were literate. But preliterate peoples compose poetry too. They just learn it by heart before it gets written down. Illiteracy never disqualified anyone from expressing his or her heart to God in psalm. So since we have far more questions than answers about the authorship of individual psalms, I've chosen somewhat arbitrarily to designate some of our psalmists here as female.

As for my choice of psalms, I'm not sure of my method beyond trying to include all the major themes covered by the Psalms. This led me to include Psalms 137 and 139, even though they're nobody's favorites nowadays, except maybe atheists'. But if we read only what sounds nice, comforts us and is easily handled, we seriously limit what the Psalms can give us. The huge diversity—even unmanageability—of the book is the very thing that grants us such potential for growth, provided we allow it to do its holy work in us.

The fact that Jewish, Catholic, Protestant and Orthodox numbering of both psalms (chapters) and verses differ one from another throws me a curve ball. I want to be as inclusive as possible, but I refuse to unduly clutter the text on my readers. In order to avoid clutter, then, I've regretfully embraced exclusivity here, as the lesser of two evils. I've chosen to go with Protestant numbering since the King James Version has made it the most familiar to us.

As already noted, at the back of the book I've included a glossary of terms the psalmists' first readers would have been familiar with, but that most readers today either won't know or may find confusing. And since there's nothing to say my chapters must be read consecutively, I've marked each glossary entry's debut in a chapter with an asterisk.

Interpreting the Psalms

It's often observed that you can make the Bible say anything you want. And the charge is unfortunately true, but only if it's some sort of divine imprimatur you seek and not God himself. "If it is true," writes Paul Ricoeur, "that there is always more than one way of construing a text, it is not true that all interpretations are equal." Interpreting the Psalms faithfully, we seek not justification for *our* views, so much as *God's* take on things—most importantly, on how we should live our lives. And that doesn't always come easy. Because it means opening ourselves up for God to read us like a book and tell us what we need most. When we do that, scripture becomes God's word to us.

None of us are very good listeners on our own. So God has to open our ears and our hearts to hear him. When he does that the idea of multiple meanings ceases to threaten. Because he can easily use a single psalm to say very different things to us at different times, facing different situations.[20] Our first goal as interpreters must be to grapple with what the text meant to its original audience. But there's always a whole range of meaning connecting it to us. And to give some idea of how that works, I've included two quite different meditations on Psalm 24.

This doesn't render all meaning fluid or suggest that contradictory meanings are valid. But neatly partitioning off a text's "fixed" interpretation from its more "flexible" application to our lives grossly oversimplifies the matter. Our postmodern friends are right to insist that meaning is far richer and more involved than that.

While the Psalter's preeminence in North American literature was secured by its being the very first book published on this continent,[21] many will question the Psalms' relevance to us today. But despite the fact that life in the 21st century differs radically from that of both the Pilgrims and of the Israelites before them, there's a timelessness about the Psalms that makes them more valuable today than ever. We have so little anymore that really roots us in the past, says Kathleen Norris, and "...as ancient as they are, the Psalms reflect our world as it is..."[22] If nothing else, that certainly does point to their being inspired poetry.

A Writer's Prayer

My one fear is that some will assume I've mastered all the truths touched on here. Fine words written about Holy Scripture can so easily suggest that. Against that assumption, I freely confess myself a novice to many of these truths. If I limited myself to writing only about things I'd mastered, my scope would be very small indeed. My hope and prayer, rather, is that the truths I write about will master me more. I write to teach, but even more to learn.

The Psalms are God's invitation to intimacy, wholeness and life in relationship with him. An invitation he extends to everyone everywhere. So I offer these reflections with the prayer that they'll help my readers receive his invitation with humility, gratitude and joy and enter in.

1

The Choice

¹How enviable are those
not swept along by the self-seeking crowd
who won't join in its empty sneering
or spurn God's way.
²They delight instead to follow the Torah.*
Drawing on its wisdom day and night
³they thrive like trees beside clear flowing steams—
bearing fruit without pause
growing old but not weak
making gains, only gains.

⁴But not the self-seeking!
They're like tumbleweed in the wind.
⁵Without a leg to stand on before God's law
they have no place among his people.
⁶Because Yahveh* stakes out
the path of those who please him
while the road the wicked choose
leads only to doom and disaster.

No one writing a guide to spirituality nowadays would start it like this. Not that the psalm isn't beautiful in its own right. It's just that ancient Israelite assumptions were very different from most people's today. For example, many today don't assume there's a right and a wrong way to live or even that we're all participants in a spiritual realm. We try to give everyone the maximum freedom of choice possible. Indeed, many are so inclusive they see no need to choose between conflicting belief systems.

By contrast, the Bible begins with the God who revealed himself to Abraham and later rescued his descendents from Egypt. Yahveh had also given his people his law, telling them how to live. And so the Psalms start with the question of how seriously to take God's law. Because it's always been easier to do our own thing than obey God's law. What could be more universal than the assumption that making our own rules offers a shortcut to the things we want? Or that making myself my own supreme judge would be easier than answering to God?

We can all think of many famous people who have made it big on their own terms, with little or no regard for God. Some of them barely conceal their contempt for him and his moral standards, letting it out in the occasional sneer. Stars of the business, sports, entertainment, artistic and intellectual worlds, these people may more or less represent the "good life" to us, a life we may wish for a bit more of. At least its power, fortune, fame and style, but without their accompanying complications. Even more, we may find ourselves drawn to their wit, intelligence and other gifts and wish we could simply belong to that elite group of people.

The problem is that the more I wish I could be like someone else—whether a public icon or simply an accomplished friend or family member—the more I unconsciously subscribe to his values. To his idea of how to look and act, her way of thinking and living. If most of the people I look up to live as if God doesn't matter, it can have a cumulative effect over time, reinforcing my natural feeling that God weighs me down, complicates my life and is something I can quite happily do without.

This has a fairly predictable result. I come to resent the "burden" of God's laws, lapse into my own self-seeking ways and quietly make myself the center of my universe. And that leads me to go along with others when they sneer at God and his laws, all for the sake of their good opinion.

Such sneering often seems justified too. The world has never lacked for self-seeking believers convinced that God needs them more than they need him. And so I join the mockers who foolishly ascribe such ignorance to God. Because contempt for others— never very far from contempt for God—offers easy respite from any challenges they pose to me.

The psalmist sees the danger of being so drawn to evil, a danger that hasn't changed over the millennia. To be rooted in God, draw on his ageless wisdom and live by his moral values has always been countercultural.[1] But the self-seeking, whether unbelievers or believers, walk a treacherous path that leads finally to disaster. Rooted in the shifting sands of merely human ways, they end up blown away, condemned, with no place in the one community truly worth belonging to.[2]

So what's easy in the short-term turns out very differently in the end. But that's not the only reason the psalmist gives for refusing the skewed values of the self-seeking, resisting the pull of their contempt for God.

He gives us three positive reasons to live a God-centered life also. True God-seekers never miss a fruit-bearing season. Untouched by drought, they're always fully alive. And they flourish in all they do. The secret of their unmitigated vigor and abundance? Meditating on Yahveh's Word, they tap into his unfailing wisdom day and night. And as a result, they grow like the lush, river-fed trees in the Garden of God.[3]

Some readers react to the stark simplicity of the psalmist's contrasts here. Is he totally unaware, they ask, of all the people who serve God but suffer anyhow? And well they might because there's not a shade of gray to be found here. Since we aren't sure who the writer is, we can't be sure when he wrote or what he knew personally of suffering. But everyone in the psalmist's day knew of Job's undeserved sufferings and of David's too. If the writer wasn't David himself, he may have had David as his king.

Regardless, he means to depict two ways of living in something akin to silhouette form. He isn't denying that gray exists. It just doesn't work in a silhouette—that's all.

But it's also worth saying that the first psalm wasn't meant to be read on its own. Together with Psalm 2, it was intended to introduce the entire collection of psalms. And while the second psalm similarly teaches that God rewards good and evil in kind, many of the 148 psalms that follow clearly show that this isn't the only paradigm at work in his world.

By making these two psalms introductory to the whole, the compiler(s) of the book meant to establish two foundational truths from the outset. Here in Psalm 1, that all our assumptions about the ease of choosing our own way over God's way prove false in the end. It's God's way that's the smart choice. And in Psalm 2, that good will ultimately triumph over evil in our world because God is in control. Only with these truths firmly in place are we ready to understand the many subsequent psalms Walter Brueggemann calls "psalms of disorientation."[4]

Every step we take moves us toward some destination or other. We may not *consciously* choose a destination, but we choose one just the same. Not wanting us to meet any surprises at the end of our chosen path, the psalmist refuses to be distracted by either the short-term benefits of the one or the short-term costs of the other.

So he assures us that the path of self-seeking leads finally to brokenness, alienation and ruin. The path of God-seeking to increasing wholeness and life in company with others grounded in him. And by the grace of God, he'd have us choose life.

Prayer

I choose you, Lord, your humble followers and the path you marked out for us. Don't let me turn away in pride or sneer my way to disaster. Humble me under your strong hand to live as you ask me to. Root me in you, so I can draw on the lifeforce of your unfailing wisdom. Because like a tree tapping into a subterranean stream, I choose you.   Amen.

2

Coronation Song

¹What nonsense!
Mere earthlings furiously plotting the overthrow of heaven!
²Kings and big shots conspiring
against Yahveh* and his Messiah.*
³Crying, "Let's burst their chains off us
and break free from these tyrants once and for all!"
⁴Enthroned in heaven above
God laughs out loud at the absurdity of it all.
⁵Then his laughter turns to fury
and his rebuke terrifies them.
⁶"Now get this," he says
"It's all over and done: I've made my choice
installed my king on Zion,* my holy mountain."
⁷That day Yahveh solemnly charged me:
    "Today I've made you my royal son
    myself your royal father.
    ⁸Just ask and I'll make the nations your coronation gift.
    Draw your boundaries around earth's remotest corners.
    ⁹You'll crush all resistance
    like an iron rod shattering a clay pot."

[10]So look out, big shots!
Wise up, wise guys!
[11]Submit to Yahveh reverently
gladly, though shaking in your boots.
[12]Quick! Fall before his son and kiss his feet
lest he destroy you while you're still deliberating.
His anger could strike any second!
But if you run to him for shelter
all that awaits you is blessing.

Behind this psalm is a startling idea. The idea that people are not just self-seeking in their pursuits, but are even hostile to God's "interference" in their lives. In fact, the kings and other leaders conspiring here are more than just hostile. They're bitter to the point of seeing God and his anointed king as tyrants. And to a degree they can no longer tolerate.

This may conform to our idea of Middle Eastern rulers as people gripped by constant rivalry. But with our media informing us daily of our own leaders' selfishness—how bent they can be on getting their own way, having everything for themselves and appearing important—who are we to cast stones? And if it's not our politicians, then it's our CEOs, university profs, religious leaders, managers and so on. So it should be amply clear that we're talking about humanity across-the-board.

Not that these same people—us, really—don't have glimmers of God's glory all over them too. Because they do. But sometimes our selfishness reaches a point where agreement on anything seems unlikely. That is, unless our shared bitterness yields unanimity on the one thing everyone secretly wants: to get rid of God and his chosen representative. Not God as a mere figurehead, mind you. That wouldn't matter. No, as meddler and the disrupter of our lives. We so hate having him tell us what to do, are so convinced we know better.

Most scholars, both Jewish and Christian, see this psalm as referring to the promised Messiah, the king whose rule would perfectly fulfill all the promises God gave to David.[1] Those promises specified that one of David's descendants would bring God's rule to its perfect realization here on earth.[2] So whether the psalm was written by David or someone else much later, it prophetically anticipated David's greater son and it did so without saying how or when it would be fulfilled.

The fact that the compiler[3] of the book made this psalm one of the two psalms introducing his entire collection argues strongly that he read it this way too. Psalm 1 contrasts the God-seeking with the God-spurning life, while Psalm 2 contrasts the king who perfectly represents God's rule with those who bitterly oppose it. The first psalm calls us as individuals to a life of obedient faith, while the second calls us to that selfsame submission as nations. And the first psalm promises God's blessing now, while the second promises good's ultimate triumph over evil. This was how the compiler chose to frame all the psalms that followed.

With this in mind, three things stand out in this psalm. First, God's "interference" in history is the problem. No one cares about a far-off God who minds his own business. The Messiah was to represent God's rule on earth perfectly. That is what his sonship to God meant.[4]

In ancient practice the overlord or emperor called the vassal king his son, indicating that he was giving him all the advantages and responsibilities of sonship. So David and the kings that came from him were all God's sons in that sense. But beyond this, the psalmist undoubtedly has in mind God's promise to David in 2 Samuel 7:14 too: "I'll be his father and he'll be my son…" In context, the verse speaks of the irrevocability of God's commitment to this Messiah-king and of the permanence of his reign.[5]

This means the Messiah represents God's "intrusion" into everyone's affairs. This is God in your face. Graciously offering amnesty to all who surrender—yes.[6] But demanding their absolute loyalty nonetheless. In response to so nonnegotiable a demand, it's no wonder his opponents unite against him.

Second, while the story clearly refers to a single king anointed by God—his Messiah—it's a universal story too. Because we're all God's daughters and sons,[7] in a very real sense we all represent him to each other.

And the overthrow of God's woman and God's man has been going on apace since Abel fell lifeless to the ground and is retold in a myriad of ways. In everything from the ageold murder of Naboth[8] to yesteryear's Holocaust or Shoah. From our corporation-spawned sweatshops and the poverty of most coffee and cocoa growers, to the veiled contempt many hold our homeless in and the Chinese villagers' birth defects from the factory-scorched earth where they live. It's reenacted daily from the nation's most opulent boardrooms to its most ordinary schoolyards, where kids are beaten up for just being different.

Though we may camouflage it well, the callous choice is always a product of bitterness, back of which stands a quiet rage against God's "intrusion," his right to tell us what to do. We may angrily espouse the atheist cause or simply shrug off "the God theory" so-called. We may piece together our own spiritistic medley or simply refuse to take God's law seriously while professing to serve him as king. Regardless, it's the same impulse that moves us in each case.

It actually makes little difference whether we reject him outright or just implicitly, in those we consider less deserving than ourselves. Our rage may not show initially. But under the right circumstance it will eventually surface unless we run to him for shelter instead.

Last, the irony here is that the autonomy we so desperately crave is the very thing that's killing us, while the submission we so staunchly withhold is the only way to blessing in our broken world. Seeking shelter in God leads to all the blessing the first psalm promised to those who obey him. Insisting on our autonomy, we become our own worst enemy since bitterness always damages us far more than the person we're bitter against. So we either continue in obstinacy, rage on and risk the king's mounting anger or we submit, embrace God's Messiah—and all God's other representatives to us—and with him the abundance of God's blessing.

The Messiah will ultimately extend his just rule to earth's remotest corners. By embracing God's rule now, we do our part to bring that to be. And with or without the trappings of royalty, what blessedness can compare with that?

Prayer

I seek shelter, God, from the bitterness that blinds me to your purity and truth. From the rage that would consume me. From myself. Free me to love as you love me, Lord. Freely, unconditionally. To cherish the least and the lost as my brother and sister—your royal son and daughter. Because what can possibly stand against a love like that? Amen.

3

Nothing Else Matters

^{1}So many enemies, Yahveh!*
Mobs massing against me.
^{2}"Even God won't get him out of this one!"
they guffaw and gush.
^{3}But you shield me from every blow
honor me with your presence
and lift up my downcast head.
^{4}I cried to Yahveh
and from his holy mountain he answered me.
^{5}I stretched out and slept
and woke up refreshed.
^{6}For with him beside me
why should I fear these enemy hordes
closing in on every side?
^{7}Move out, Yahveh! Save me, God!
Yes, you'll hit my enemies' iron jaw
smashing their bared fangs
^{8}because victory belongs to you, Yahveh
and your blessing to your people.

David's life was anything but tidy, antiseptic. Tradition has it that he wrote this psalm at one of the messier points in his life, fleeing from his egomaniacal son, Absalom. If that's true, then the psalm leaves out a fair bit I wish David could have processed here. For one thing, the ambiguity of his love for Absalom. There's no denying he loved him deeply. But so conflicted was he over his son's evil actions and his own evil reactions that he was barely on speaking terms with him and the whole topic walled off to discussion.

What happened is that Amnon, Absalom's half-brother, raped his sister, and King David, their father, let it slide. When Absalom avenged Tamar's rape by killing Amnon, David banished him and later very reluctantly allowed him to come home but not to see him. When he finally granted him his long-awaited audience, it was a superficial fix that addressed none of the issues.[1]

David says nothing here about the roots of the conflict that's overtaken him. I guess it would be a lot to ask him to sift through all its mutual contempt now. That would come later unfortunately.

When we understand all that's going on, though, David's sins* against his son look minor. Because Absalom wants, not just his father's crown, but the head it sits on too. And the masses that once swore themselves to David, celebrating his exploits with gleeful abandon[2] have just as readily dumped him for a man who, having murdered his brother, now wants to take out his dad too.

A veritable Greek god, Absalom is the newest face to simultaneously grace the covers of *Time, GQ* and *People* magazines. And if he's learned anything, it's the importance of image, talking a good line and working the crowd. And the worst thing about working a crowd is how well it works if you know what you're doing.

Having sown to the wind, David certainly reaps the whirlwind here as Absalom slowly leaks out to the nation all the patricidal bitterness he's stored up over the years. So no one but David—preoccupied with all his own stuff—is surprised when it takes full expression in Absalom's attempted coup.[3]

But David doesn't mention Absalom's name here. We might see David's hurt over the masses' abandoning him in the psalm's opening lines, but his focus isn't there either. It's limited to just two things. The deadly threat staring him in the face and then Yahveh, his comfort and strength in the midst of it. If the threat facing him is the screen David puts up for us in the psalm, then Yahveh more than fills the screen for him.

I don't usually think of God as localized, belonging to one hilltop or another, but David did. Yahveh had made David's capital city his home on earth. And that essentially put the gateway between heaven and earth on Mount Zion.* So living there as God's designated king made David the recipient of God's unstinting blessing, provided he listen well and obey. But like most of us, David did a lot of other things way better than listening and obeying. And this psalm finds him running, not only from his home, but also more seriously from the site of Yahveh's presence and blessing. David surely wouldn't have struggled to answer the doggerel "If you feel far from God, guess who moved?"

Being hunted was nothing new for him. He'd survived King Saul's nerve-wracking game of cat and mouse for years. But that was then. Now he's the older guy in the chase and most of the country has signed on with his enemy. The problem he's left to simmer quietly all these years has now exploded before the nation. Making a mad dash for cover with your bloodthirsty son in hot pursuit is terribly humiliating. So he might have assumed along with everyone else that he'd lost God's favor too. Indeed, so black and white did the situation look that his enemies couldn't help but indulge in premature gloating.[4]

But no sooner does David cry out, than God—gracious, compassionate—comes running. And not with a sermon or lecture on his many sins either. He simply comes. Although David has every reason to lie awake or lapse into fitful, broken sleep, he stretches out and sleeps like a baby, secure in the knowledge that Yahveh, the Invincible, stands between him and his enemies. What difference if they're counted in tens or tens of thousands, are far off or right now closing in on his tent? With Yahveh, the great deliverer, on his side,[5] none of that matters.

His sins may wreak bloody havoc on his family and his people and shut him away from his beloved son. But not from Yahveh. Nothing can separate him from his relentless love. Yahveh protects him, honors him with his presence and lifts up his head. So his focus changes from how far his stocks have fallen, to how present God is for him now. Since it's the one thing everything else answers to, it's really all that matters. So he sleeps and wakes up refreshed, alive to God and the present unfolding in his hands.

David ends by asking for help, on the one hand, and declaring his faith, on the other. The time for action has come, so he asks God to move out against his foes just as his foes have moved against him. And no sooner does he make his request, than he declares his confidence. He sees God hitting them, totally putting them off the chase. Because what kind of hunter is a lion with broken teeth? He sees Yahveh as the winner too—the lion who having gotten his prey, shares his bounty with all his dependents. The nation has been torn apart by Absalom's rebellion, but David trusts that God's blessing will bring healing again. And so it does, but not as David expects. God does rescue him from his son and restore the nation to him. But Absalom dies in the process, leaving David to wander that whole walled off area of his life alone.[6]

His beloved son's death will always remind him that what you sow you one day reap. But brokenhearted though he is, David discovers anew the truth that God's warm embrace is enough for every new present we face. While it doesn't necessarily erase the past, it does free us from it, releasing us to live afresh in the all the fulness of God's blessing.

Prayer

You love me relentlessly, Lord—never leave me nor forsake me. Though I mess up times beyond counting, you still hear my cry, shield me from my enemies, put your arms around me and rescue me from disaster. Please help me give you the same undivided attention you give me, Lord. Make me your worthy child, I pray. Amen.

6

Cry in the Dark

[1]Enough punishment, Yahveh!*
Enough tongue-lashing!
[2-3]Pity this poor weakling and heal me
because anguish runs right to my core
so that even my bones shudder.
How long, Yahveh?
[4]If you really love me
look down and save me before it's too late.
[5]What good am I to you dead and buried?
Will I sing to you from my coffin?
[6]I'm worn out crying—my pillow awash with me
on the salt sea of my tears.
[7]Blinded by tears, I grope
in the darkness my enemies have unleashed on me.
[8]Back off, you agents of evil!
[9]Yahveh has now heard my cry and answered my prayers.
[10]That's right: before they know it
my enemies will be red-faced fools
fleeing for their lives!

Without the laws of science to buffer things for them, the ancients lived in the immediate presence of their gods. Proximate causes notwithstanding, defeat, sickness and every other kind of national or personal misery were lumped together under the category of the gods' displeasure.

The same was true of the ancient Israelites, except that they had only one God to anger or please. This allowed their prophets to speak clearly about what pleased and displeased him. By contrast, the neighboring gods' multiplicity often left you unsure of just why you were being blessed or cursed.

Not so with Yahveh. Blessing always came from keeping his covenant,* cursing/punishment from breaking it. At least, that was the theory. The problem was that it didn't always work. But before we go there, a couple of notes on how we get on with the ancient worldview.

We have two real problems with it. First, we feel lost in so wholly religious a world. We want God much more in the background, leaving *us* to deal with germs, family psychology, weather patterns, market trends and all the other proximate causes, as if he was only remotely involved. We feel safer with God as a company figurehead who lets us take care of the business of living ourselves, asking only a passing nod of respect. Someone who may be able to help us if we're really stuck—or maybe not.

But however we feel, this isn't remotely biblical. When you think of it, how much is such a God really worth? And what guarantees that our culture has its worldview right, succeeding where so many others have failed? Biblically, we either embrace theism full on—meaning that God takes center stage—or else believing in him is pretty useless.

Our second problem is with God's rebuking and punishing, like we're little kids needing a spanking. But the psalmist clearly believes God is punishing him, though God is not doing the actual drubbing. He either commissions or permits—and the line between them is rather hazy—our enemies, seen as agents of evil, to inflict their torments.

Again, we must accept God as God and grant him the right to discipline us as he sees fit—trusting that he does so only for our good—or else demote him to demigod status purely for our comfort. The psalmist clearly has no thought of doing that. So when he commands his enemies to back off, he does so because of his assurance that God no longer backs them, having apparently switched sides.

Biblically speaking, all this makes sense. It's as common in the rest of the Tanakh* as in the Psalms.[1] Isaiah 10:5-27, for example, gives the same sequence of events. There God promises to destroy the arrogant Assyrians, but only after using them to punish his people. All this was in fulfillment of Yahveh's warning that he'd send a nation down on them like an eagle, brutal, "with no concern for either the elderly or infants."[2]

Psalm 6 doesn't give us any specifics, but it does fit squarely within this framework of blessing and cursing. Verse 7 alludes to God's warning in Deuteronomy 28:29 of anguish so deep it leaves his people groping at midday like a blind man in the dark. So much is clear. In the psalmist's imagery, his enemies' determination to destroy him suggests that God is so carried away that he almost beats him to death. Put off by the harshness of this imagery, we might recast it in terms of God's having us take an extended "time-out," but how well would that really convey the psalmist's pain?

This brings us to the fly in the ointment of covenant's retribution thinking. Quite simply, things are not always as they should be. Sometimes God-haters are blessed and God-pleasers cursed. But scripture's oldest book, the book of Job, addressed this, saying that we're just too small to grasp all God's ways.[3]

Job also suggested something we see over and over in the Torah,* Psalms and Prophets. That God isn't just the God of retribution. He's also the God of reversal. He not only grants mercy to sinners, but allows the pure of heart to suffer also.[4]

Though reversal is not spelled out in the black and white legal terms that give retribution its edge in the Torah, it's no less vital to covenant relationship.[5] Indeed, since mercy and grace are about God's granting us the welcome we don't deserve, how could he make any covenant with us at all apart from reversal?

One thing this dual paradigm does is give the biblical worldview a depth it wouldn't otherwise have. Seeing this keeps us from a common mistake that goes with operating under one paradigm only, that of retribution or reciprocity—that doing good brings good to us, while doing evil brings evil. The mistake I refer to is the common assumption whenever anything goes wrong, whether of small or tragic proportions, that the sufferer must have sinned. Our marriage breakdown, our brother's job loss and our friend's cancer, all point unerringly to the victim's sin or debilitating lack of faith.

But with two paradigms operating simultaneously, God alone can say which accounts for the blessing and which for the suffering we see around us. In fact in our twisted world, it's no less likely that blessing or suffering comes to us undeservedly as deservedly. Naturally, undeserved blessing is far easier to take than undeserved suffering. It's also right to cry out to God in your suffering, whether it's undeserved or not.

So the psalmist tells him his miseries and acknowledges they're from him. But the remarkable thing is that he does so without pleading either guilty or innocent. He may actually be doing something quite sophisticated. Where we expect either confession or protest, he gives us only the sound of the breakers crashing on the sea of his tears. Neither confessing nor denying his guilt, he thus plunges us with him into the silent terror of his growing darkness by day, till the "how long?" of verse 3 echoes in every breaker's crash.

Whether he feels his punishment is deserved or not, he responds by crying out to the only one who can call his enemies off. And ever gracious, God finally hears and grants him relief.

Prayer

I so often don't see you as I should, Lord. But though my worldview all too handily holds you at arm's length, you're still present in every joy and every pain I feel. So help me to live in your presence, cry to you in my pain, embrace your inscrutable wisdom and believe that, however severe, your discipline is forever good. Amen.

7

God of Justice, God of Truth

[1]Help! Save me, Yahveh,* my God!
I count on you for shelter
[2]lest like lions, my stalkers grab me
drag me off and rip me apart
with no one to hear or help.
[3]If their charges are true, Yahveh—
[4]if I've turned on a sworn friend
spitefully helping his enemy—
[5]then let them get their quarry, mow me down
and grind my honor into the dirt.
[6]Burst onto the scene, Yahveh!
Meet the fury of my foes
with the inferno of your anger!
See that justice is carried out!
[7-9]Summon my accusers to stand before you
and let all rise as you take your seat
high above all earthly courts.
Then, Yahveh
you who probe us all heart and soul
pronounce me innocent, faithful.
Be the God of justice you are

and ring down the curtain on evil
replacing its henchmen
with one who will reign under you in faithfulness.
[10]The High God is my shield
saving all who sincerely seek him
[11]judging justly on behalf of the faithful—
his anger against evil burning constant.
[12]Whenever anyone refuses to repent
God sharpens his sword
and silently pulls his bowstring taut.
Even now his strong arms are tensed,
[13]ready to release his flaming arrows
with perfect accuracy!
[14]But having given himself to darkness
my enemy conceives evil's dark plans
labors to deliver them and gives birth to lies.
[15]Yet in hiding his trap for me
he's only setting himself up!
The deeper he digs his pit
the farther he'll fall when he stumbles into it.
[16]His violence will crash back down on his own head.
[17]How grateful I am that
Yahveh always comes down on the side of right
and so I sing praise to him as God Most High!

Many today want to believe in a God of justice, but doubt they can. They see the horrors of the Rwandan slaughter with its evil colonial roots, horrific cases of sexual abuse, fraud in high places, racial prejudice and evil systems that bestow untold misery on whole classes of people, all the ways they themselves have been used and abused, and they say, "Why can't God just balance a simple ledger… if there is a God?"

Personal injustices often cry more insistently for answers

than larger social issues since you stand alone, misunderstood by everyone. And being falsely accused—what prompts this psalm—is one of the hardest injustices to bear.

Tradition has David writing this when a relative of King Saul accuses him of spitefully helping his sworn friend's enemy.[1] That would mean the sworn friendship was with Saul, the one guy in the country who held the power of life and death in his hands.

Ancient Israelite society was a network of polarizing friendships where, magnet-like, becoming Saul's friend automatically made all his friends and enemies yours. Key friendships were formally sworn and were what kept you in power if you happened to be king.

So for anyone to accuse you of pretending to be the king's loyal friend while secretly aiding his foe was enough to threaten not only your career in his court, but your life too. Worse still, David is accused of doing this simply out of spite. This accusation may have been the proverbial last straw, prompting the insanely jealous Saul to lead his army out to scour the country for David, his supposed enemy.

No wonder David begins here panicky, breathless, terrified. That we might expect. But what strikes me is how certain he is of God's justice. Theoretical atheism was never a big draw in David's day. People went straight from life's injustice to God's indifference and then—importing a full cast of gods caught up with us in evil *en route*—concluded that life is just very complicated. If you strip away the clutter of gods in that view of things, it's still very attractive today.

But David doesn't question God's justice or love or look anywhere else for help. Instead he engages in some wonderfully therapeutic prayer. We need to recognize, though, that that doesn't happen in a vacuum. His thoughts are shaped by three things the Torah* has God saying an unwavering *yes* to.

God's first *yes* is to our humanity. For us to make real choices in a moral universe, God must allow us the freedom to go wrong. If he always took over for us just as we were about to mess up, we'd have a much tidier world, but our choices would all be meaningless. Because the instant we chose selfishly God would override our choice with his instead. But God wasn't prepared to give up our full humanity—our freedom/responsibility—not even for a perfectly just world.

God's second *yes* is to mercy. Thankfully, part of his response to Adam and Eve's sin* was to defer the full effects of its death penalty.[2] His mercy intervened to grant our race a reprieve—a very long one, as it turned out—in the hopes that we might turn around. But our being able to choose selfishly without his instantly zapping us means many innocent bystanders get hurt. Sometimes tragically so. We hurt ourselves too. And like it or not, it's all because God is committed to redeeming our broken world.

God's third *yes* is to holiness. He shows no favoritism whatsoever and has committed himself to punishing every selfish act, regardless of how religiously connected the actor is or how many "brownie points" she's saved up by doing good deeds. He's not taken in by surface appearances either. He holds the guy who nags his wife or is stingy to those in need responsible for his sin regardless of his churchgoing, work ethic or community service. God's holiness makes all sin intolerable and guarantees that every ledger sheet will indeed be balanced and everyone falsely accused vindicated at the end of the day. However unlikely it seems now.[3]

But God doesn't promise to nab the worst offenders now, deferring everyone else till judgment day. No, he refuses all our accelerated timetables. Because in an effort to make him look more just, they actually end up compromising his holiness—his right to be God and do as *he* knows best.

So although thugs are running the country and David is running for his life, he chooses to trust in God. Faith always is a choice, after all, and often not an easy one. It's always easier to lampoon God than offer a better alternative.

With his heart tuned to truth, David chooses God and runs to him for shelter. He sees his enemy laboring to take his fraud from conception to living, breathing reality and he sees God, who has grown angrier by the day, standing poised and ready to strike him down. Yet while David asks God to enact justice and declare him innocent without delay, he knows it's not up to him to decide. In fact, his full vindication before the nation takes many years to happen.

In the meantime, though, David sees God shielding him from harm and bringing his enemy's evil crashing down to crush his own head—because evil does ultimately have a way of doing that. He sees a God he knows he can trust to come down on the side of right. And having caught his breath, David sings. For the clearer our vision, the more we overflow with praise to God unfathomable, all-glorious—God Most High.

Prayer

Lord, I don't understand your ways—am often flat out winded by the suffering and injustice you allow. But though I hate to say it, as I hear your *yeses*, I see no better way. And so like David, I choose you and cry out for your justice and aid for the weak and oppressed. And with David, I praise you for being the just God that you are. Amen.

8

Such Wisdom, Such Wildness

[1]Yahveh,* our Lord
your wisdom, power and love
shine in every leaf and stone and blade of grass!
Your glory outshines suns and stars past counting!
[2]And yet you've chosen little children —
mere babes at the breast —
to champion your cause and silence your bitterest foes.
[3]When I look at the star-strewn skies above
it's the work of your fingers I see —
the moon and stars you made.
[4]Who on earth are we, mere humans
that you care for us?
Why give us a second thought?
[5]But you made us the very pinnacle of your creation
with only you above.
And you crowned us with glory and honor —
[6]lords of the earth —
putting everything under our feet:
[7]sheep and cattle on the hillside
lions and wolves in the wild
[8]every bird that flies the skies above

and every fish that swims the seven seas.
⁹Yahveh, our Lord
your wisdom, power and love
shine in every leaf and stone and blade of grass.

We've always had our skeptics, but opposition to God can take many forms. In the psalmist's world, everyone believed in the High God who had created everything. This was the God who called Abraham and revealed himself to Moses by the name of Yahveh.

The problem with Yahveh, though, was the exclusive bit. He claimed absolute authority over everything and called for a devotion no less absolute. Submitting to Yahveh required you to throw out all the stand-in gods thought to take his place. You either walked past all those lesser gods to embrace him alone or you made the High God into a sort of absentee landlord—the guy who may own the place but never bothers to show up—and dived headfirst into that wild carnival of gods before you.

The great thing about a carnival is its in-your-face immediacy. It may not be classy. But it is colorful, loud and exciting. Same thing with most idolatry.

Your deepest fears of sexual or personal inadequacy confront you everywhere? Embrace a sex god. Their sacred prostitutes waited on every hilltop to confer the god's fertility/virility, success and power on you. Poisonous snakes threaten your family's lives? Placate the serpent god. The river beside your house threatens to overflow its banks? Sacrifice to the river god.

The gods were never easy to get along with, but at least they were right there in front of you: as real and as close as sex, your fears, the storm, the river. Leaves, rocks, grass and you-name-it, all manifested one or more of the gods.

But with such a muddle of gods to deal with, idolatry's cure was worse than the disease. For example, who was responsible for a storm at sea? The storm god, the sea god, the sun god—who clearly wasn't showing his face—or some stellar god who controlled things from afar, like the moon controls the tides?

So gods there were aplenty, everywhere and in everything. Whatever you did throughout the day put you in direct contact with a whole myriad of them. But sorting out which one was demanding your undivided attention at any given point was a task too big for even the gods. So you just did the best you could and took your lumps whenever you got it wrong or one of the gods was having a bad day.

The psalmist's vision here is radically different. Far from seeing the gods, it's Yahveh's wisdom, power and love she sees in everything around her. Everything from a newborn's first cry to the entrancing brightness of a super galaxy—all expresses him.

I love her tone here. Yahveh's detractors were everywhere, but she refuses to get defensive. Why defend God when everything in creation argues so persuasively for his presence right here, right now? Why argue the obvious?

So instead of defending his immediacy, she celebrates it. She celebrates Yahveh in sun, moon and stars and she marvels at who he's chosen to champion his cause. Little children! The sweet simplicity of an infant's charmed gurgle or a toddler's delighted squeal proclaims God's wisdom, love and power with an eloquence no skeptic can equal.

Even the baby's gentle cooing at her breast is enough to silence God's bitterest enemies. He also reveals his truth to little kids. Sweetness and simplicity no more take away from truth than eloquence and sophistication make up for fraud. That's why God isn't remotely threatened when his cheering squad turns out to be a frolic of youngsters chanting his praise.

One thing idolaters ridiculed was the idea that the High God would actually take an interest in us—humankind. "Who do we think we are to warrant the avid attention of so great a Creator?

How pompous can you be?" So they just made do with the gods.

The psalmist doesn't argue that point either. She essentially says, "You're absolutely right. It is crazy. And if that isn't wild enough, Yahveh's given us the whole farm—entrusted the whole earth to our care!"[1]

But mind-blowing though that is, which is more pompous—to accept what God says, childlike, or to philosophize him to the periphery of our lives in order to somehow *look* humbler? What kind of humility is it that denounces the grandiosity of the biblical vision only then to take center stage and push God off into the wings?

We insist that all our objections are logical—that no intelligent person could think otherwise. But as Pascal so wisely said, "The heart has its reasons which Reason knows nothing about."

And isn't that one of the biggest differences between children and adults when it comes to God? We think up 25 objections to God's reality for every affirmation of truth we hear. Kids, on the other hand, don't give such reasons room to get in the way. If God says he made us in his likeness and entrusted his treasured creation to us, then so it is, however incredible it seems.[2]

This only leads the psalmist to ask, "What made you do it, God? Why would you even give us a second glance?" And the only answer she comes up with here is the awe and wonder she began with, celebrating again the God whose wisdom, power and love shine so bright in all she sees around her. Really, what more can she say?

Prayer

I can't think why you'd entrust your world to us, Lord, especially knowing how we'd squander that trust. Nor why our failure only made you open your arms wider to redeem us and our world. Give me eyes to see you in earth and sea and sky. And a heart to love you and your creation fiercely, freely, with your own wild abandon. Amen.

9

God of Impossibility

[1]I thank you, Yahveh,* from the bottom of my heart
for all the awesome things you've done!
[2]I celebrate you, High God, and sing your praise.
[3]Dropping like flies
my foes gave up the chase when they saw you appear.
[4]You defended and judged with perfect fairness—
upheld my cause, [5]blasting the nations*
and destroying all who sold themselves to treachery,
blotting out their names for good.
[6]They burnt out like lights, never to be relit again—
like the cities you wiped off the map
whose names no one even remembers—
[7]while Yahveh reigns on as king forever.
Calling heaven's court to order,
[8]he judges with perfect justice for all.
[9]He's the shelter the broken run to when in trouble.
[10]Which is why all who know Yahveh
put their confidence in him.
He never deserts anyone who turns to him.
[11]So sing your praise to Yahveh
who reigns from Zion.*

[12]Tell everyone how unfailingly
he hears the cries of the weak
and having seen everything
avenges their blood.

[13]Be gracious to me, Yahveh!
See what my enemies are doing!
Snatch me away from the gates of death
[14]to burst through Zion's gates
with news of how you've saved me.

[15]The nations who rejected you
have fallen into the pit they dug for me—
[16]their feet tripped on the very net they hid for me.
You took them down when they least expected it, Yahveh.
[17]Oppressors always end up dead
just like all the nations who forget God.
[18]Because at long last you remember the desperate
and downtrodden, fulfilling their hopes.

[19]Move out, Yahveh!
Don't let these small-time thugs defy you!
Make the nations face your stern judgment now.
[20]Strike terror into them, Yahveh—
remind them that they're just puny men![a]

We see two contradictory things in multiple images here. The psalmist confidently praises God for guaranteeing him justice and rescuing him from the degenerates out to get him. He sees his pursuers giving up the chase as soon as they see God is on his

----
[a] The poetic form of Psalms 9 and 10 argue strongly for their being treated as one psalm. But for reasons of space, I've chosen to deal with them separately.

side.[1] With all the winning numbers in hand, what fool would turn down a chance like that?

But just past the psalm's midway point, he gives us his second picture. One fleeting look over his shoulder and the psalmist tells us how desperate he is right now—how close to dying, how far from home and the streets he longs to fill with the happy news of his deliverance.[2]

No sooner does he cry out to God, though, than he sees him remembering the poor and throwing his enemies into the pit they dug for him. Clearly, the psalmist refuses to exercise his faith at the expense of reality. If his enemies' shadows utterly dwarf God now, he knows shadows can be like that. It's all about perspective. So he asks God once again to show them who he is by judging them now.[3]

What amazes me here is not that the psalmist holds two opposing views, but rather how freely he moves between them. It reminds me of the Queen's candid admission to Alice: "Sometimes I've believed as many as six impossible things before breakfast." But when you think of it, the psalmist's ability to hold faith in tension with reality is the very thing that makes it worth having.

At the same time, it's what makes it so hard. I can live with a God who answers my every prayer just like I think he should. Or if I must, I can accept a God who can't do much about the evil running rampant in our world. That was how many of the ancients saw God—too preoccupied with his own stuff to be bothered with theirs. No one likes that God. But at least we can write him off and get on with the business of looking out for ourselves as best we can.

The problem comes when on the one hand I have to face the reality that it's not all about me and God isn't intervening— with its clear implication that he may *never* intervene— while on the other hand I must still believe both that he's able to do whatever he wants and that he genuinely cares too. Waiting on such a God is hard. Waiting indefinitely and with unflagging hope impossibly hard.

While the psalmist's faith picture has God righting every wrong committed against his people, that's certainly not where he finds himself now. Bloodthirsty degenerates are chasing him even as he speaks, smack dab in the middle of a situation where God hasn't shown up to rescue him on que.

Still he refuses to take that to mean that he won't come through for him. He sees Yahveh, High God though he is, hearing every cry the marginalized utter—essentially sheltering every battered wife, comforting every abused child, caring for all the hungry.[4] But he knows only too well that wrongs are committed against the oppressed[5] and with shocking regularity too. That God's love and power often don't translate into the vindication and blessing we think they should. So the psalmist lives with a tension that is at times almost unbearable.

Yet as hard as it is, this is the only kind of faith worth having. For God to right every wrong and heal every disease the moment we ask him or "claim it by faith" might seem to prove incontrovertibly that he cares. But it also turns God into a glorified vending machine in the sky and faith into a magic carpet that rides your every wish to wherever you want to go.

I must admit, some days that's all I want. But in the end, it's reality we must come to terms with. And what could be clearer than that the biblical record is rooted in this unflinchingly gritty reality from start to finish? True, it's thoroughly infused with the supernatural. But as Rabbi Kushner says, sometimes faith itself is the biggest miracle of all.

Frankly, despite its shallowness, I love the false sense of power vending machine religion gives. But isn't the goal to be growing into God's moral likeness? And why would we need to do that if our every prayer was answered? It would mean we always knew what we needed and never needed God to correct our thinking. And that would make us gods in our own right, which is the master lie behind every empty fantasy we entertain.[6] It certainly isn't where this psalmist lives and moves and has his being.

He says, "Yes, you hear every whimper and are fully committed to righting every wrong. It's all true... but it doesn't feel true now. I can see you doing it—it's that close—but it hasn't happened yet. In fact, I'm *this* close to death. So please act on my behalf before it's too late!"

Faith is never either/or. It's always both/and. Always its distinctive mark is letting God be God in the real world. But that's also the hardest thing about it—honestly facing reality, yet refusing to let it diminish God's power, justice or love in any way.

Prayer

Lord, I love how honest the psalmist's faith is. I just hate it that you require the same honest faith of me. Yet that's exactly what you do require. So help me not to trade reality for faith—nor faith for reality either—but let you be God and cry out in my desperation. Even if it means believing six impossible things before breakfast. Amen.

10

Who Are the Poor?

¹Why are you avoiding me, Yahveh?*
Why do you disappear when I need you most?

²In their arrogance, evildoers chase down the poor.*
Make them victims of their own devious schemes, Lord!
³They boast about their desires as if they already had them.
They applaud the greedy and scorn Yahveh.
⁴Their pride leaves them no room to seek him
so they push him right out of their minds.
⁵Yet they're consistently successful, grow haughty
and scoff at anyone who opposes them—
all without the least concern for your laws.
⁶They all tell themselves:
     "Nothing bad's gonna happen to me—
     I'll never have anything to worry about!"
⁷They intimidate with curses, lies and fraud.
Mischief and evil well up from under their tongues.
⁸They lurk on the edge of town
stealthily watching the innocent
waiting to get their victims alone and murder them.
⁹They hide like lions ready to pounce on the weak

to catch them and drag them away.
[10]Overpowering their victims
they leave them crushed and broken.
[11]They assure themselves:
 "God's looking the other way.
 Oblivious, he doesn't see what I do!"

[12]Do something, Yahveh!
Stretch out your hand to judge!
Don't forget the downtrodden.
[13]Why do the wicked think they can dismiss God
with an offhand, "Nah, he couldn't care less"?
[14]You see everything, God!
You track their evil and will judge it all!
The poor commit themselves to you
because you are the helper of the fatherless.
[15]Break the striking arm of the wicked!
Go after their evil till there's none to be found!
[16]Yahveh is king forever and ever.
The nations* will one day be gone from his land.

[17]You hear the heart-cry of the humble poor, Yahveh
and will grant them courage till the day when
[18]you champion the cause of orphan and oppressed
and mere mortals terrorize no more.

The question "Who are the poor?" brings words like *welfare bums, freeloaders* and *low-lifers* to many people's minds. Even if we don't say them out loud.

 If that's true of you, you probably got your opinion from your family, which is how most prejudice comes to us—*a priori*, as beliefs we accept without knowing the facts. Basically, our families point our "antenna" in a certain direction. And we go through life picking up anecdotal evidence to support our prescribed prejudgments.

We meet someone who won't work even though he could or who collects welfare and works under-the-table too. And we take the fact that *some* poor people do this as confirmation that *most* poor people do.[1] But if I've learned one thing from working with homeless people, it's that provided their health permits, most of the poor really do want to work honorably.

We meet a mom who has no food for her kids but has brand new furniture, a big screen TV and the latest electronic gadgetry— all thanks to the miracle of plastic. And we conclude that *most* poor people wouldn't know what to do with more money even if they had it. But why blame the poor for learning budgeting the hard way—or not at all—when our self-indulgent consumerist society goes so far out of its way not to teach it?

Most of the homeless I know actually do as well as middle class people when it comes to budgeting—some well, some badly.[2] The big difference is that the margin of error in budgeting is so much narrower when you're poor.

We see someone battling alcoholism or drug addiction, someone whose life choices preclude the stability needed to build a normal life. And we decide that *most* poor people wouldn't change even if we paid them to. But if we deny the chemical basis of addiction, then we truly are ignorant. And our penchant for labeling people—e.g. "alcoholic," "loser"—may actually be the biggest reason they don't seek the help they need.

Three things are true of all prejudice. First, it relies on the skimpiest of math, facts and logic to produce its stereotypes. All of our *mosts* above become fixed in our minds without reference to any real statistics or critical thinking.

Second, prejudice minimizes distinctions within groups we're hostile to and maximizes distinctions between "us" and "them." The poor are just as nuanced as any other large social grouping.

But we paint them all with one brush.

And last, prejudice loves smokescreens and red herrings. "We're *always* going to have poor people with us…" is a common one. In other words, why bother helping them? But why then wouldn't the same logic apply to the elderly or disabled?

Another is: "Compared to places like Burundi, we've got no poor people at all." The idea being, if our so-called poor would just stop whining and complaining, they might actually be able to improve their lot in life.

But while Burundi's poor easily make North America's poor look well cared for, looks can be deceiving. Not being able to feed your family hurts no matter where you live. Not having money for rent at the end of the month is nerve-racking whether you owe $10 in Burundi or $1000 in a G8 economy.[3] And if you're poor, getting sick or being hit with unexpected expenses—e.g. your work tools are stolen—is brutal no matter where you live. Admittedly the worst of Burundi's poverty defies description and we must do all we can to help. But that hardly means no one whose circumstances are any less tragic can be called poor.

The tragedy here is that so many otherwise good people hold such jaundiced views of poverty. People so busy insisting everyone play by the same rules that they're blind to the huge systemic setbacks the marginalized suffer even in relatively classless North America. Biblically speaking, they're so smug about their own hard work, good stewardship and God-given success, that they're blind to anything that challenges their self-righteous view of themselves. Yet if we listen to the prophets, God sees their arrogance as worse than the laziness they presume to judge.[4]

That unbelievers view the poor like this is one thing. But it's something else when believers see life and consequently read scripture through a lens of unbiblical moralism, one that insists we all get what we deserve in life. Most of us have been raised to see things this way: the jobless poor, the sexually abused, the imprisoned, the abandoned or otherwise disgraced—if we knew *all* the facts about them, we'd see they actually "had it coming to them."[5] It's this hard-edged moralism that allows us to spiritualize the poor right off the page wherever we see them in scripture, to turn "the poor" into "the spiritually needy." God isn't fooled by the games we play, though. The tragedy is that we so often are.

Our North American affluence puts many of us at a disadvantage because it lets us believe the myth that we actually deserve what we have. The reality is that every good thing we have is a gift. Neither is human evil slight or superficial. Biblically speaking, it's truly radical and a good deal of the evil that comes to us is undeserved. We must see two paradigms at work here, not one. Reciprocity tells only half of the story, reversal the other half.

The psalmist speaks of the faithless deliberately going after widows, orphans and the poor.[6] He calls on God—their defender—to take their side against their oppressors.[7] And he melds poverty and humility together in verse 17. These poor humbly cry out to God for help and protection just like the psalmist does.

Scripture presents a balanced view of poverty. The psalmist is no communist, pitting rich against poor. Social class isn't the issue at all. Living like God doesn't care how we treat the poor is.[8] On the one hand, the Tanakh* pictures the lazy poor who need nothing better than a good dose of reality. Who squander what chances they have and complain as if they'd had none to squander.[9]

But it also sees the many poor who don't deserve their plight. Political refugees like David under Saul. Abandoned moms raising kids without their dad. Kids growing up without a parent. It refers to them when it says, "If you plug your ears to the cry of the poor, you too will cry out and be ignored… If you exploit the poor, you show contempt for their Maker… If you care for the poor you lend to the Lord."[10] The poor matter a lot to God. They, no less the rich, are made in his image.[11]

The psalmist says God will one day repay all who oppress the poor. What about those who simply ignore the poor? Who show little-to-no compassion as the poor struggle to rebuild their broken lives? People whose very inertia can be so damning? The psalmist doesn't say. But surely in the context of the Tanakh, contempt for the poor, *whether active or passive*, is contempt for God.

Prayer

How easily my smug view of myself makes me refuse to see how many of the poor don't deserve their poverty. Forgive me for turning away in arrogance. You'd have me think and feel as you do, Lord. Not just grudgingly or self-righteously do "my little bit" for the poor. Give me your heart for the poor, I pray. Amen.

14

Of Scoundrels and Fools

[1]Fools rule God right out of their lives.
Polluted of soul, they yield to impulse
choose badly and commit deplorable acts.
[2]Yahveh* looks down from heaven
to see if he can find anyone anywhere
with enough sense to seek him.
[3]But every last one of us has missed the turn
and abandoned the path.
We've all fouled ourselves horribly.
No one chooses right.
No one.

[4]Don't these scoundrels who never pray to Yahveh
yet routinely prey on his people
[5]know how soon terror will grip them?
Because God always sides with those who seek him.
[6]You foolishly think you're going to trash
the dreams of the weak and vulnerable.
But no, Yahveh will shelter them.

[7]Oh, how I wish Israel's deliverance

was on the way right now from Zion!*
Because when Yahveh turns things around
for Jacob's sons and daughters
we'll sing and dance for joy.

The fool hath said in his heart, There is no God. So goes the Authorized Version.[1] And for years I read it as a description of people like Sam Harris and Richard Dawkins, who deny the existence of God. But I'm afraid the folly the psalmist speaks of is far bigger and more insidious than *theoretical* atheism. Still we can take that as our starting point here since it is related.

Not all theoretical atheists oppose the *idea* of God. But all dispute the *particularity* of Yahveh or any other God. Because that's where God asserts, invites, demands and we become part of *his* story, like it or not. It's where even entertaining the possibility of Yahveh admits that saying *no* to him might not actually make him go away. This leaves us like children who aren't asked if we want to join in the game. Play we must and by these rules and no others. And for some, that turns God into a despotic taskmaster right out of a Dickens novel.

But if this autocratic aspect of theism infuriates atheists, equally aggravating is the insensitivity many traditional and fundamentalist theists promote their closed-case religion with. Ironically though, insensitive religious dogmatism often breeds its perfect irreligious like. So the two sides may well be even in terms of evangelistic aggressiveness. Dawkins and his cohorts can be as dogmatic and preachy as any fundamentalist.

Jews, Christians and Muslims all have history to be ashamed of—times when we've been aggressive to the point of treating fellow believers, let alone unbelievers, like objects to be acted upon instead of hearts to be won. But likewise, Lenin, Mao and their successors have ruthlessly crammed atheistic dogma down the throats of millions. So it is mindlessness—whether theistic or atheistic—on so all-embracing a subject as God that diminishes and degrades our humanity.

Biblically, faith and unbelief are relational. It's not primarily that we hold a set of beliefs or keep a set of rules. It's that God created us for love. And like all true loves, this love requires trust and makes rigorous demands of us. But still it's love for God that's at stake, not merely a creed or list of dos and don'ts.

Loving my wife includes such things as honoring her, keeping myself for her sexually and doing things as mundane as picking up my socks and washing the kitchen floor. Because I love her I want to please her. Love always involves shared beliefs, values and boundaries. But we only lose by exchanging mere boundaries for the love they were meant to protect.

So in the context of his infinite love, God invites each of us to play a lead role in *his* story, a story of unmatched beauty, depth and breadth. Not only that, it's the very role we were made for. He also invites us to discover a love and freedom that transcend all else—to see him in our brother, sister and the creation around us, to discover ourselves in discovering him.

But this is where the story goes wrong. Preoccupied with our own lust for power, pleasure and greatness, we've all of us veered away from the path of self-fulfillment God set for us, onto paths of increasing smallness and self-sabotage. And not just once or now and then. An element of selfishness and pride actually taints all we do. Till God strains to find anyone who gets it right and sees him as our true home. But he finds not one.

We all play the fool, exploiting others when the mood takes us and we think we can get away with it. Some even make a career of abusing others, themselves and God.

It's actually this *functional* atheism—the mother of all atheism—that the psalmist has in mind. Forgetting my place, I grant myself an *ad hoc* license to rule my universe, effectively pushing God out of the picture. And I do it without fuss or muss, renouncing neither morals nor creed. Consciously, that is.

Of course, unconsciously I renounce all each time I choose selfishness over God's way. Which is what makes functional atheism so insidious. I can slip in and out of it 100 times a day, all the while presenting only my best side. And not just to the world at large, but far worse, to myself. So I may think I'm on course and even champion the route I say I'm on, while God only knows how relentlessly and how perilously I'm being pulled out to sea—away from him.[2]

Verses 4-6 speak of people blind to their need of Yahveh, scoundrels who ruthlessly prey on his people. In all their momentary power, they forget something truly unique about Yahveh's rule: his fundamental solidarity with the poor and weak, the marginalized and broken. So with absolute certainty the psalmist promises a day of reckoning and reversal when the dreams of the powerless will come true and all their oppressors be overthrown. And already he delights to think how God's people, who cling to him for mercy, will dance for joy on that day.

Who then are the fools he speaks of? Actually, who aren't they? We all foolishly play God and each in our own way can be scoundrels too. But like Jacob, as soon as we see our lostness, we can call on him to save us. Because while Jacob was a scoundrel in every sense of the word, he did see how desperately needy he was on his own. He did know enough to cry out, "I won't let you go until you bless me."[3]

That's really all that distinguishes medial from terminal human folly. Never seeing their need of God, some people live entire lives of godless folly. They may be outwardly religious, going through the motions of calling on him. Or they may embrace the delusion that they can avoid hypocrisy and self-centeredness simply by shunning organized religion.

If only it was that easy! The irreligious fail to live up to their morals and ideals and present false pictures of themselves just like the rest of us do. When it comes down to it there is really only one difference between us and that is that some of us see we can't live truly without the God of Jacob, while others, mistaking someone else for him, never do.

Prayer

Lord, you know us inside and out. Open our eyes to what you see—image of God yet broken beyond our mending. Longing for you, our true fulfillment. Yearning, yet relentlessly pulling away too. And in our lostness, Lord, grant us the holy desperation that cries out, breathless but unyielding: "I won't let you go until you bless me!" Amen.

15

The Trouble With Goodness

[1]Yahveh,* who gets to live on your holy hill
as part of your royal court?

[2]Those who live with integrity
do what's right
and are honest with themselves and God
[3]Who don't slander
wrong their neighbors
or turn a blind eye to their families' sins
[4]Who hate sleaze artists
honor God-fearers
and follow through on their promise to punish evil
[5]Who don't take advantage of the poor
or rob the innocent of justice for a bribe.

Whoever lives like this will never be ousted.

A friend of mine—I'll call her Alana—is divorced and a recovering
addict. Now halfway up the North Face of change before her, she
wants to "give her life back to God." But the church she grew up
in leaves her feeling shut out, second-rate.

This makes me want to weep. Why wouldn't every church welcome her as the VIP she truly is? Why can't we see that God meant churches to be hospitals for the soul, not the exclusive religious clubs we turn them into?

This psalm puts the focus where it should be because goodness is what God is all about. Not goodness in the abstract. No, the practical, shoe-leather kind that alone can change the world. And not mere external piety either. Any scoundrel can produce that. No, Yahveh puts honesty, integrity, kindness and justice at the core of his moral requirements.

The trouble with morality is its exclusiveness. There's a good side to this because we all want to live in a world exclusive of evil, violence and contempt. But we so easily marry that exclusivity to our false assumption that God won't accept us till we're all cleaned up—basically perfect.

As a result outsiders to church, synagogue and mosque typically feel shut out by members in good standing who they feel silently condemn them. Sadly, they're often right there. But why do we do that? What could possibly make recovering patients look down on untreated patients? That they're better *off* than them is obvious. That they're *better* than them is not.

Only if we miss biblical faith's central plank—that God's mercy is ours by sheer gift—do we harbor such miasmic exclusivity. Scripture undeniably sets down standards to govern the behavior of those in the community of faith. And all who persist in spurning those standards must be excluded—its leaders especially. Otherwise we'd have no hope of redemptive community. But the Bible nowhere suggests that people must attain those standards in order to gain admission.

So this twisted exclusivity resides not in morality *per se*, but in the ignorance and pride by which we credit ourselves with moral superiority. Biblically speaking, even the best among us is nowhere near good enough. So the moral standards God sets for us are meant to drive us into his open arms. We have no hope of meeting them without his grace empowering, his wisdom guiding and his community embracing us.

But how easily we forget that and take credit for what God does in us. From there our fall is swift as pride of grace bars us from grace itself, leaving us to fall back on our own goodness. And that's never enough to meet the moral challenges put to us each day. So we're left covering an empty and unsatisfying spirituality with only the appearance of grace.

The fact that God continues to work with us in such perversion is entirely to his credit, not ours, and shows how passionately he loves us despite our brokenness. But again we typically take it to mean we've earned his seal of approval—that we really are good in and of ourselves. Ironically, we can fall prey to this spiritual pride even while claiming to be trophies of his grace, masking self-righteousness and selfishness with the foul pretense of both goodness and humility.

In *The Matrix* Morpheus says, "…there's a difference between knowing the path and walking the path…"[1] Saying everyone should live a certain way while departing from it ourselves is hypocrisy. And the higher we raise the ethical bar, the greater our temptation to spiritual fraud—whether the embarrassingly obvious or the more subtle kind.

The import of this is profound. Namely, if living like God wants us to live typically puts us more at risk of hypocrisy, not less, then any call to goodness that doesn't warn of that heightened risk leaves itself wide open to spiritual shallowness. The Bible has a lot to say about this inbuilt problem, but not every scripture does. Though I hate to think of it, I know I've lapsed into hypocrisy repeatedly over my lifetime—probably over the past month too. And a seemingly endless number of forms is available. None of us consistently lives up to our own standards, let alone God's.

We may never consciously embrace hypocrisy. But we all

have a seemingly endless capacity to "lie with sincerity," as André Gide put it. And a big part of that lies in our projection of hypocrisy onto others, making it external to us. This is understandable because who wants to own such pervasive brokenness as this? But seeing hypocrisy as the problem of others limits us to surface morality, leaving the heart of the matter alone.

The psalmist will have none of it. His list of qualifications begins with integrity, doing what's right and being honest with ourselves and God. It's not about doing what merely *looks* right, but what *is* right. The level of integrity he calls us to is no less daunting than the North Face Alana is scaling.

We grow best when we're being honest with ourselves and God. Honestly listening to him keeps us from slandering, backstabbing and being unkind. It also frees us from the appeal of God-despisers, binds us to other God-seekers and makes us take evil seriously.

Taking the psalm to be asking who God appoints to his royal court—in democratic terms, his cabinet—is my own interpretation. But as I write this, the world waits to see who President-elect Barack Obama will appoint to his top executive posts. We do this with every newly elected leader. As we wait, we ask what kind of people she's looking for, something no one knows better than the leader herself.

The same question was asked of ancient kings and queens too. So why not of Yahveh, Israel's ruler over all? Besides being the sacred site of Israel's worship, Yahveh's temple was also his residence and the site of his royal government on earth—his "White House," so to speak. Living in his home "on his holy hill" meant eating at his table, being part of his royal court.

If I've got that right, then the psalm would have applied first and foremost to Israel's royal court and leading priests. But this was actually the measure Israelites, one and all, were to aspire to because all were called to serve Yahveh their king. To actualize his will in their lives and spheres of influence as he enabled them. So we can read the psalm in terms of that broader calling too, as the psalmist asks and answers what Yahveh requires of all who serve him.[2]

What a relief to know that this is the goodness our God calls us to. And that none who live like this will ever fall from his favor.

Prayer

You are light and you are love, dear God. Not in conflict, but in perfect harmony. When will we be like you, as gracious as we are truthful? Help us to welcome every Alana who seeks your mercy and exclude none but those who spurn it. Flood our lives with your goodness, Lord, that we may love what you love and hate what you hate. Save us from ourselves, we pray! Amen.

19

The Fear That Frees

[1]The skies announce the glory of God—
the high-vaulted heavens beyond, his artistry's grandeur.
[2]Each day discloses his power and wisdom anew.
Each night picks up where the night before left off.
[3]Though without sound, word or syntax
[4-5]every broadcast is crystal clear and gets perfect reception
the whole world over.

With all the glow of a bridegroom on his honeymoon
the sun emerges each morning
from the tent of stars God pitches for it.
Then like an ironman from the starting line
[6]it blazes across the sky, from one horizon to the other
leaving nothing untouched by its ferocity.

[7]Yahveh's* Torah* is true soul food:
words so reliable they make the naïve wise
[8]directions so just they make the heart soar
commands so luminous they open eyes
[9]fear so pure it lasts forever
rulings right and true, every one.

¹⁰Words more alluring than mountains of pure gold
more delightful than a hatful of strawberries
picked in the wild.
¹¹Words warning your servant of danger
and beckoning to rich reward.

¹²But who of us can detect his own blind spots?
Free me from all the sins I'm blind to, Lord
¹³and strengthen your servant against the insolent—
don't let them overpower me.
Then I'll be whole again
free from their monstrous rebellion.

¹⁴May my every word, my every thought
be just what you want
Yahveh, my Rock and my redeemer!

Few today think of any sort of religious fear as liberating or life giving. But we speak of having a "healthy fear" of whatever poses a real threat—say, radiation. Fear is deemed healthy when it shows us our limits and protects us from hidden dangers. And nowhere is that more vital than where something is good and dangerous at the same time. Electricity, for example.

Yet for many people, transferring the concept over to the religious sphere automatically strips it of anything healthy. We associate religious fear with the fanatics who gave us 9-11. In Christian terms, with Jonestown-type cults and guilt-tripping hellfire harangues. Going further back it conjures up images of Salem's witch trials and the Spanish Inquisition, making us shun it as a tragic perversion of goodness and faith.

But as well-founded as our distrust is, it's only half right. Because the selfsame enemy back of such aberrant faith is at work in us too and is no less insidious. I refer to the inborn selfishness that makes us want to always get our own way, be right, be the center and look good no matter what. We may want to be free from all such pettiness, but it isn't within our power to free ourselves from it. Because how can self cast out self?

I see other people's lapses far more easily than my own, which often blend right into all my best attempts at doing good. How can I avoid what I can't see? I make progress in one area only for selfishness to rear its ugly head in another. So it's often one step backward for every two forward.

That's why, despite its very real potential for distortion and abuse, the fear of God is at the heart of this psalm and at the heart of biblical faith rightly understood. Nothing enables us to see our need of grace quite like encountering what Rudolf Otto called the *Mysterium Tremendum*, the God whose presence is at once honey to our souls and yet is overwhelming, even terrifying, in its awe and power.[1]

The question really is *how small of a God do we want?* Because unless we want a God shorn of all majesty and mystery—reduced to our puny size—we do want the fear of God. Smaller gods cannot free us from ourselves and make us whole.

But like any other fear, the fear of God is only communicated secondhand to a point. Beyond that, staccato repetitions of dire warning by fellow sinners—especially those in authority over us—all too easily lead to the sort of distortion that sucks us both into a vortex of spiritual abuse.

Encountering God myself eliminates that. Whether I want to hide with Adam and Eve in Eden, tremble in awe with the Israelites at Mt. Sinai or exult, enraptured, with the psalmist over God's Word, my fear is rooted equally in Love's implacable intolerance of evil and in its wholly unexpected grace to me.[2] This truth backlights all the psalmist says here.

In his world the sun was widely worshipped as the god of justice. So he acknowledges the sun's terrific warmth, beauty and power in the sweep of its daily course. But however divine it may seem, it attests only to the greater majesty of its maker, who is in fact the God of justice. And as awe-inspiring as the sun is, it is mute beside Yahveh's very own words in scripture.

Lovingly instructing, warning of danger and promising rich reward, the Torah is designed to bless God's people and keep them from ruin. But presumptuous and headstrong as we all too often are, we spurn the wisdom and love behind God's warnings till we're overpowered as Cain was. Because evil has designs on us no less than it had on him.[3]

This carelessness is the very thing the fear of God stands against. Yet how pervasive such spiritual torpor is in our day. Nor is it surprising when secular humanism endlessly intones that no one—not even God—can decide what's right for us or how we should live our lives. And what music that is to our ears!

Two distortions in our culture make the god-like status this confers on us more challenging still. First, we encourage reckless freedom—pornography, "uncomplicated" sex, living on adrenaline, recreational drug use, divorce-for-any-reason and other high-voltage items—refusing to see that such freedom disables even as it thrills. We proclaim this hedonism as normal, harmless, smart and enlightened and we lampoon all dissenters as narrow-minded traditionalists and bigots.

Next, we extol tolerance, or at least our brand of it, above all else and hypocritically shame anyone "arrogant" enough to believe differently—for example, that the overarching story told in scripture is true for everyone. But why then shouldn't skeptics be equally condemned for saying scripture misleads everyone? Why does holding to fixed moral standards— that all worship should be reserved for God, for example— have to mean *imposing* them on others? Why wouldn't insisting on moral relativism be judged equally intolerant?

Believing these lies, we resist the powers of darkness only

feebly, ignore Love's dire warnings and succumb to encroaching evil. If only we could see our motivations as clearly as we think we do. But pride is self-deception. While some sins are plain and obvious to us, many are insidious, hidden until God opens our eyes.

With such treachery afoot, what more could we ask than to rediscover the freedom the fear of God can bring? However its opponents attack, belittle or shun it, nothing else can keep us from falling prey to evil in this dark day like the holy fear that prompts the psalmist to pray as he does. Urgently, lovingly, with all his heart.

Prayer

Surely being our own final authority on right and wrong is no less rebellious than the idolatry of the ancients. We've rejected your liberating fear, God, and forgotten our place. Please forgive us and strengthen us against such monstrous evil. Free us to walk humbly before you, our every thought and word just what you want. Amen.

22

For the Abandoned of the Earth

¹My God, my God
why have you deserted me?
Why are you always out of earshot
however loud I roar?
²All day I call out but you don't answer—
nor do I let up the whole night long.

³Yet elusive as you are
you're at the heart of Israel's* worship.
⁴Because you're the one
who rescued our ancestors when they trusted in you.
⁵You saved them when they cried to you—
you never stood them up.

⁶But look at me, worm that I am.
Subhuman, a blot on the earth!
⁷All who see me shake their heads
taunt and sneer.
⁸"He trusted Yahveh*
so now Yahveh's got to save him—
he's so obviously pleased with him!"

⁹Yet you're the midwife who brought me out of the womb
and laid me at my mother's breast.
¹⁰My caregiver from birth, Yahveh,
you've always been my God.
¹¹Don't hide from me
now that trouble has found me helpless and alone!

¹²Monstrous bulls rage and snort on all sides.
¹³Ravenous lions roar in my face, jaws gaping.
¹⁴I'm spilt like water on the ground—
bones unhinged, heart melted like wax
¹⁵strength shriveled to nothing
tongue stuck to the roof of my mouth
here where you've laid me out in the dust of death.

¹⁶This gang of thugs closed in like wild dogs
ravaging my hands and feet.
¹⁷I look down and count my bones, one by one
while all my enemies look on and gloat.
¹⁸They divide my clothes among them
throwing dice for them.

¹⁹Don't turn away, Yahveh—
you're all I have left!
²⁰Run to my rescue before the sword takes me!
From these slavering dogs
these roaring lions, ²¹these raging bulls
save me! save me! save me!

²²Then I'll tell all my brothers and sisters
what you've done—
praise you before everyone at worship.
²³I'll say,

"Praise Yahveh, all you God-fearers!
Give him glory, sons of Jacob!
Revere him, daughters of Zion!*
24Because he didn't shun
the destitute with all his troubles.
He didn't turn away aloof
but heard my cry for help."

25My praise will overflow
and when the whole community meets for worship
I'll keep my vows to you:
26the poor will feast to their heart's content
and all who seek Yahveh
will praise him for his bounty and say,
　　"May you all live like this forever!"

27The whole world will hear
what Yahveh has done and turn to him.
Every people on earth will bow low in worship
28because all power and authority belongs to Yahveh
who reigns supreme over the nations.*
29From earth's poor and destitute
on up to her rich and powerful
all will bow in worship before him.
30On hearing what Yahveh has done
their children will give their allegiance too.
31They in turn will announce
his *coup de grace* to those yet unborn—
the good news of all he's done.

God-forsakenness wears a million different faces, whether on
John Steinbeck's migrant workers or Francis Ford Coppola's
lost soldiers.[1] Edvard Munch gives us another in "The

Scream." While Annie Dillard, reflecting on a child's face badly burned in an airplane crash, sees God as a glacier in whose shifting crevasses we live unheard.[2]

As unfamiliar as these images would have been to the psalmist in his vastly different time and place, their soul-chilling terror was all too familiar. He is attacked by enemies who now happily watch him, naked and bereft as his life ebbs away. He roars at the God who refuses to answer him by day or night, fearing lest he's stretched him out on the ground for burial—lest he too is just waiting for him to die.[3] So he copes with the agony of abandonment by counting his protruding bones, while his enemies gamble for his clothes, utterly blind to the pathos before them.

But as shocking as their inhumanity is, the problem of God's seeming indifference looms larger still. Could God possibly be as nonchalant about the psalmist's pain as his sneering, smirking enemies? No, the psalm's ending eliminates that possibility. Because the psalmist knows the character of Yahveh, he knows God cannot abandon him. And since Middle Eastern parties are always over-the-top affairs, the psalmist imagines himself passing on to the poor a small taste of God's lavish generosity to him—in food, song, dance, laughter and the warmest welcome imaginable.

Whether or not David wrote the psalm as tradition has it, we're given no clue as to which story the psalmist recounts. Regardless, its ending is remarkable. Ecstatic over his last minute rescue, the psalmist extends Yahveh's righting of wrongs across the board as small and great, rich and poor, in every nation under heaven bow before Yahveh. He also sees his story being passed from one generation to the next, making it as timeless as it is universal.

Couple the messianic overtones of that larger-than-life ending with the way Jesus identified himself with the psalmist's God-forsakenness here, and you can see why Christians read this psalm prophetically.[4] Which is all fine as long as we remember that the psalmist told his own story first of all.[5] Since all true

images of God-forsakenness ultimately adhere as one, why would
the psalmist need to know who else he was describing for his psalm
to apply to them too? The object of racism, the AIDS victim left
to die alone, the abused wife, should all see themselves here. Nor
did he need to know who would best picture God-forsakenness to
our race. Inspired poetry always speaks to far more than it knows.

But to share the psalmist's ecstasy, we need to see how very
countercultural his rescue was. Left to die alone in the dirt, the
chance such a "worm" had of receiving the personal care of
an exalted ruler in the ancient world was nil, underscoring the
psalmist's fear. You sure couldn't count on the gods—who
characteristically outshone their subjects in treachery—for grace.
But thankfully, High God though he was, Yahveh had committed
himself to the weak and the poor and was faithful to his word.

Although God's rescue is yet future for him, the psalmist's
delight in it is so real that we can't imagine it not happening.
Somehow his putting all his imagined testimony in past tense—
"Yahveh didn't turn away aloof"[6]—makes it just as real to us as
the pain that precedes it. So although we don't actually see
his deliverance, we feel like we have. And the fact that many
centuries later, we too have been drawn into the story and fulfill its
prophecy anew with each retelling[7] makes it that much surer
to us.

Is abandonment always guaranteed this sort of deliverance?
No, the psalm can't be made to say that. But even so, it does
offer incredible hope. Because the psalmist's confidence assures
us of God's undying compassion for the poor and weak. Of his
constant commitment to us even in the soul's dark night and of his
ultimate righting of every wrong.

Prayer

Lord, everything is out of whack down here, broken. But the news that you're the One who will finally sort it all out, that you love us however far we fall in the eyes of others and are on our side no matter how deserted we feel—that is good news indeed! So help me to gladly share its bounty with the poor, as being myself one brought back from the dead.   Amen.

23

Shepherd Song

[1]With Yahveh* as my shepherd
what more could I want?
[2]He lays me down in lush, green fields
leads me beside spring-fed streams
[3]and renews my strength.
Good shepherd that he is
he guides me always in the true path.

[4]Even walking through the valley
where Death's dark shadow reaches after me
I fear nothing with you beside me:
your crook and your club, they comfort me.

[5]You spread a rich feast before me
in full view of my enemies
massage my head with fragrant oil
and pour my cup brimful of blessing.

[6]Your goodness and mercy chase me down
every day of my life
and Yahveh's house will be my home

for days and years without end.

Last night my wife and I started out for an appointment in good spirits, glad to be together, glad to be going out. By rights, we should have had enough time to get to our destination comfortably. But the traffic was way heavier than usual and none of my best efforts to go faster helped.

Add to that the fact that Cathy and I have a long history of me making us late and her hating to be late and you can imagine how my frustration grew as I sensed—or imagined—Cathy's growing annoyance over what was happening. False guilt and anxiety pulsed through me each time I thought of it, pushing my stress level up: *It shouldn't be like this! now what's gonna happen? we're gonna be late and she's not gonna like it! you should be going faster... shoulda left earlier... It shouldn't be like this! now what's gonna happen? we're gonna be late and...*

Halfway there the obvious broke into my broken-record mindlessness: *No matter how I watch for an opening, the traffic is simply going way slower than I'd like. I've prayed we'll get there in good time but, barring a Back-to-the-Future-type miracle, it ain't happenin'!*

Suddenly worrying about a situation I couldn't change made no sense. We were where we were—comfortably ensconced in the present, not dangling precariously between an unchangeable past and an uncontrollable future. Wishing we were somewhere else wouldn't change a thing. I simply needed to stop *should*-ing on myself, accept reality as it unfolded—all my limitations in space and time included—let God be God and just be present. Content right where I was in the traffic.

Then it hit me how much energy I waste resisting reality, chafing against it. That I truly embrace the unfolding future only to the degree that I accept my present situation and live in the moment.

That insight calmed me briefly. But as I negotiated city streets a few minutes later, a concrete barrier where I needed to turn left saw me uselessly railing, only to realize I was doing it again. I had to ask myself: *If this is the way the road goes, how will my anger change it or give me the extra minutes I crave?* And seeing how chafing against reality throws me into turmoil, I remembered Jesus' insistence that each moment's challenges are all I need to think of.[1]

I gain nothing by importing problems from either my imperfectly remembered past or my imperfectly envisioned future, both being equally beyond my grasp. Refusing to accept what's true about me, my situation or others around me is just another way I try to help God run the universe. As if he needs my help!

By contrast, contentment frees us to be fully present where we are now, fully alive to our emerging future. It means accepting everything about ourselves: strengths, weaknesses, abilities, limitations, past history, wants, needs, resident good and evil, guilt, innocence, naïvety, confusion, fears. Not necessarily liking them, but acknowledging and owning them. Resisting reality only makes things worse. Contentment begins by accepting reality equally for what it is and what it's not—accepting our situation and everyone around us—letting them be. That position frees us to think, pray, listen to God and then believe and act like he really is God.

What has all this to do with Psalm 23? Everything. People most often draw on this psalm's rich comfort when death confronts them with its loss and its loneliness. The psalm's nearly standard use at funerals has made it the world's best-known and -loved poem. But the psalm speaks to far more than just bereavement. The death of someone we love inevitably forces us to accept reality as it is—not as we think it should be—and so affords us a gigantic chance to let God be God. But we were meant to live our entire lives knowing that God is here for us now. A concrete barrier blocking your way will do just as well as bereavement—thank-you very much.

What life is not full of frustrations as Murphy's Law reasserts itself with all-too-frequent regularity? But surely we're meant to be present to everything our good shepherd leads us through. Not wait till our next funeral to recall that he's here for us now. Because if faith only comes through for us in life's hardest losses, if it doesn't also deal with all the everyday hurts and frustrations in between, how helpful is it?

And isn't resisting the pain itself half the pain? Letting God be God makes his way far easier. Because in contentment, we see everything differently. Though many hillsides we graze aren't that lush, we see the richness of his mercy.[2] Surrounded by malicious enemies, we're amazed at how boldly God takes our side, spreading a feast to encourage and strengthen us.[3] Though our way isn't problem-free, our good shepherd's care is meant to make it worry-free. He's there for us when the friend we counted on betrays us, the company we gave heart and soul to terminates us, the beloved family member dies or a simple concrete barrier blocks us *en route* to an appointment.

I so often think I'm in control of my life and really need God only for those exceptional times when I'm not. But it's all a myth. About the only thing I'm in control of is my response to a situation. Beyond that it's pretty hit-or-miss on my end. The shepherd's crook and club are always in his hands. And that gives me such comfort because I know the unfailing goodness of the One who holds them. Knowing my own weakness and unreliability, I'd be a fool to wish they were in my hands instead. Yet I'm afraid I do with shocking regularity. As if that would bring me peace.

I also find myself thinking the world's dysfunction and pain are elemental, constant, real. But far more basic still are God's goodness and grace, which pursue me relentlessly. They, not my circumstances or my false sense of control, are the basis of my peace. They will remain long after all the world's brokenness and pain are gone. My true home.

Freedom, abundance and peace are all internal conditions that depend on nothing but our good shepherd's unswerving commitment to us. Without them, no amount of anything can truly satisfy us. With him on our side, we're freed from debilitating fear, freed to be all he meant us to be, freed to live life to the full despite its brokenness and pain.

Prayer

I choose to be right here where you have me now, Lord, content to be me. Not chafing that I'm not somewhere, something or somehow else. Not weighed down by the past or needing my future to somehow validate my present. Not rushed or harried, however fast I'm going. Calm in your commitment to me. Overflowing with praise. Amen.

24a

Freedom in the Face of Fear

[1]The earth is Yahveh's* and everything in it—
the whole world and all who live in it.
[2]Because it was Yahveh who made solid ground
rise up out of chaos—
brought dry land out of surging ocean streams.[a]

[3]Who can ascend Yahveh's hill
and stand in his holy place?
[4]The clean of hand and pure of heart
[5]who haven't bought into deception
or signed on with falsehood.
[6]They'll receive Yahveh's blessing
and deliverance from the God who saves them.
This is what the company of God-seekers is like
who seek Yahveh's face with Jacob.

[7]Stand tall, archway!

---

[a] Informed by ancient understandings, the text actually refers to a three-storey universe, with heavens above and the earth founded on—not just emerging from—primeval sea.

Swing wide, you age-old doors
so the King of glory may come in!
[8]Who is the King of glory?
Yahveh, bold and brave!
Yahveh, heroic in battle!
[9]Stand tall, archway!
Swing wide, you age-old doors
so the King of glory may come in!
[10]Who is the King of glory?
Yahveh, captain of heaven's armies—
he is the King of glory!

Nothing incites fear quite like chaos. As I write this I face major challenges in three vital areas. Work, church and family. Two months ago I began a new job and still feel overwhelmed by all I have to learn in it. And the fact that I've had neither office, desk nor computer of my own—all necessary to my work—has multiplied the challenge as I've had to move camp hour-by-hour, from one space to another while my new office is being built.

Also two months ago, our church of the past 11 years called a number of urgent meetings to deal with challenges we were facing. Then suddenly, unexpectedly, the doors closed on our congregation. Now bereft of its support, we must find a new church home.

And last but not least, two months ago my aging father's health went into rapid decline and has been one continuous string of crises ever since. So most nights when I'm not sleeping at my parents I return home very late. I know I can't do this much longer, especially with everything else coming at me—that having Dad live at home crisis-free may already be an impossible dream. And I wonder why I've been blessed with such chaos. In my darker moments, I wonder what I've done to deserve it or what God's got against me.

But the fact is, our world is broken—and all of us with it. Even our best intentions fall short. So I might better feel confused by the fact that such chaos isn't the norm for my life. Still I find myself battling a creeping fear—this sinking feeling in the pit of my stomach—that I'm not going to make it and I wonder what the fallout will be if I don't.

Of course, fear is part of the human condition, however gifted or powerful we are. We face overwhelming challenges. Hostile people determined to use us or undo us. Relationship issues sometimes threaten all we value most. Intractable problems. And these aren't just random things. There are spiritual forces behind them far bigger than what we see.

We fear because we're broken, often face our challenges alone and sometimes feel haunted by loneliness. We frequently think we know more than we do, entertain inflated pictures of ourselves, make mistakes and act selfishly. Sometimes past failures come back to haunt us. Because we've been wounded, we fear and become defensive. We try our best to shield ourselves from failure, loss and shame, but there are no guarantees.

However oblivious we may be to our fears, others know why we shop compulsively, always insist on being right, drink so much or whistle in the dark. We keep our fears at bay through endless activity, empty religion and a zillion other things. But all our addictions only *seem* to make things better, numbing us to our fear as the chaos closes in.

Though it never specifically mentions it, this psalm speaks powerfully to fear because it's all about chaos versus control. We typically think of creation as something being made out of nothing. But the ancient Israelites thought of it as order being imposed on chaos.

Canaanites believed their god Ba'al had fought and subdued the god of chaos—*Yam* or "Sea," also called *Nahar* or "Stream"— to establish order in the world before ascending to reign from his mountain residence. So this psalm affirms that it was Yahveh, not Ba'al, who imposed order on the watery chaos of formlessness—verse 2 uses both *yam* and *nahar*—to give shape to our world.

In ancient Israel, those words also implied the threat of chaos the hostile Canaanites and their gods[1] constantly posed. But as earth's creator, Yahveh remains owner and controller of everything and everyone on earth. Since the threatening chaos cannot ultimately win, we needn't give in to fear.

We need only fear God and violating his moral order, which is what verses 3-6 talk about. Pleasing God is supremely a matter of lifestyle choices. Living as we please and giving him only token ritual worship will never do. He hates evil and knows our thoughts and desires no less than our words and deeds. Only as we walk before him in purity and truth are we granted his blessing and salvation.

But if those terms aren't far-reaching enough, the list ends with not giving ourselves to emptiness—implicitly, the chaos of evil and idolatry around us—and not being taken in by the world's self-serving lies. These are the people God accepts. Seeking his face, they're delivered and blessed as Jacob was.

Not that salvation isn't a gift of God's grace. Scoundrels like Jacob lay hold of this holy God and his deliverance no other way.[2] But receiving his grace invariably changes us, reshapes us in his likeness. So if the things listed here aren't increasingly true of our lives, then it's not grace we're looking at.

The psalmist ends with the all-conquering Yahveh approaching the city gates, which he commands to swing wide in welcome. This may allude to the day King David welcomed the Ark of the Covenant—the empty, portable golden throne[3] representing the invisible Yahveh—into Jerusalem. Annoyed when God didn't do things his way, David held the Ark at arm's length in Jerusalem's outskirts. But that decision made Yahveh remote and kept David from receiving his full blessing.[4] Seeing his mistake three months later, he welcomed his king with joy.

Wanting God to revolve around us means seeing the chaos confronting us as impossibly big—whether David's unruly kingdom ringed by hostile enemies or my three-way work, church and family challenge. And that leads us to panic on some level and so to live lives shaped by it, lives that can't embrace God as we were meant to.

That's why the psalmist calls us all—even whole cities and nations—to fling wide our "gates." Because we only prove the greatness of our triumphant king's wisdom, power and grace to the degree that we open our lives to him. Personally, this means entrusting my workplace, church life, family, friends and everything else to him. Submitting myself and everything around me to him as king. Not to the gathering darkness, threatening chaos or stalking fear, but to him. Though I don't know how everything will turn out, I can still live in hope because he has triumphed forever.

Prayer

You, Lord, can't be bribed or bought with offerings or prayers. Instead you've given yourself to me that I might give myself and my world to you in return. So help me refuse the threatening chaos and gladly welcome you as king. Fill my life with your goodness and glory, I pray. Amen.

24b

The Earth Is the Lord's

¹The earth is Yahveh's* and everything in it—
the whole world and all who live in it.
²Because it was Yahveh who made solid ground
rise up out of chaos—
brought dry land out of surging ocean streams.ᵃ

³Who can ascend Yahveh's hill
and stand in his holy place?
⁴The clean of hand and pure of heart
⁵who haven't bought into deception
or signed on with falsehood.
⁶They'll receive Yahveh's blessing
and deliverance from the God who saves them.
This is what the company of God-seekers is like
who seek Yahveh's face with Jacob.

⁷Stand tall, archway!

ᵃ Informed by ancient understandings, the text actually refers to a three-storey universe, with heavens above and the earth founded on—not just emerging from—primeval sea.

Swing wide, you age-old doors
so the King of glory may come in!
[8]Who is the King of glory?
Yahveh, bold and brave!
Yahveh, heroic in battle!
[9]Stand tall, archway!
Swing wide, you age-old doors
so the King of glory may come in!
[10]Who is the King of glory?
Yahveh, captain of heaven's armies—
he is the King of glory!

Climate change poses an opportunity and a threat like nothing ever before. We see glimmers of greatness as our race begins to act as one and find our way through the maelstrom. But huge negatives also abound.

Thanks to its Athabasca tar sands, Canada now ranks second in world recoverable oil reserves, after Saudi Arabia. But that's hardly good news since recovering every single barrel of Athabascan oil releases 176 lbs/80 kg of greenhouse gases (GHGs) into the atmosphere. The tailings dumped in the process are horrific too, producing toxic "ponds" so big they're visible from outer space.

And though Canada has repeatedly promised to reduce its emissions, it's still the world's eighth largest emitter of GHGs and third in per person emissions. By comparison, China's per person GHG emissions are one-seventh the average Canadian's. And Canada plans to increase tar sands production dramatically.

As a Canadian, this grieves me deeply. I'd love to hang all this profligacy on our present government, the first to put its faith in corporate junk science's take on climate change.[1] But for decades now successive Canadian governments have made promises they haven't kept. Canadian as it is to profess concern for the environment, our record consistently shows that earth's health means far less to us than our own economic growth.

The reason? We've bought into the oversized North American lifestyle. Large cars, trucks and SUVs take us from ever larger centrally-heated suburban homes to spacious workplaces and malls. Our year-round diet includes lots of CO_2-producing beef and dairy, to say nothing of fruit and veggies shipped in from afar. Most other goods come from abroad too.[2]

While we know this lifestyle degrades the environment, we downgrade our excesses either by citing "reputable scientists" who dismiss the whole idea of climate change or by fingering others more prodigal than ourselves. But at the very least "We're running an uncontrolled experiment on the only home we have," as Bill Collins put it.[3] And barring future immigrants, who among our brothers and sisters in the Two-Thirds World can ever hope to live like us? The rising middle class in China and India is now decimating tropical rainforests in its mad pursuit of our suburban life.[4] But how is our pursuit of it any saner?[5] If everyone on earth lived like us, what would be left of our planet?

Yet we live as if we have a right to our standard of living — however much of earth's limited resources it consumes — and leave earth's poor to live on handouts. Former Prime Minister Lester B. Pearson promised that Canada would lead the fight against global poverty by contributing 0.7% of its GNP to humanitarian aid. But we've never even come close and give less now than we did then. Nor has Canada ever paid more than lip service to the ONE Campaign's call to release the world's poorest nations from crippling debt. We struggle to find even a modicum of compassion for those whose earth we're spoiling.

The truth is that every lifestyle choice we make is ultimately environmental in scope. Whether we live in the city or the burbs, grow produce organically or using petroleum-based fertilizers, generate power using fossil and nuclear fuels or renewable energy sources. Whether we buy the throwaway products marketed to us or resist needless waste output, buy local or imported goods. Whether we modify organisms genetically or treasure and protect earth's precious genetic heritage. Whether we limit the size of our families or procreate with no thought of the world's fast-dwindling resources.[6]

Environmental choice is simultaneously socio-political, economic, moral and spiritual. Letting others make our choices for us doesn't absolve us of our responsibility.

Admittedly these are hard things to say and hear because who here is without sin? If only we could just tweak things slightly, it would be alright. But having made series upon series of choices with little thought of others—whether now or in the generations to come[7]—we easily feel overwhelmed by the changes we must make.

Yet cherishing what God gave us in sacred trust really matters. Well might Chief Seattle have asked how we could buy the land anymore than the sky. We may have deemed him a fool at the time, but how very wise he seems in retrospect. Genesis clearly teaches that we are earth's stewards, never its owners in the ultimate sense of the word. The earth is the Lord's and always will be.[8] So every step in the right direction counts.

Sadly, like Christian advocates of slavery in the 1800's, many right-wing Christians today twist the scripture to their own ends. But the command to "subdue the earth" was never about grinding the earth under our heels. It was always about owning our responsibility as stewards. About living thoughtfully, exercising the same care for God's green earth that he put into creating it and doing so in hope.[9]

As passionate as the worldwide environmental/social justice movement is, saving the planet is way too big for us on our own. Even all of us together. But it's not too big for the God who made earth and is still in charge. We must live out of our hope in him.

Without that, some people dream of finding a new world

like our colonialist forbearers before us. But should we ever find another living planet to inhabit, Marilynne Robinson wryly observes, "…nothing in our present state of consciousness would save it from the abuse that threatens to kill this one."[10] Others dream some miracle technology will allow us to consume the earth and have it too.

This lust to escape scot-free from the hell we're making earth to be also accounts for the mass popularity of the Christian pulp fiction series *Left Behind*. But featuring a Jesus who comes to teleport the faithful home to heaven and then incinerate our ravaged planet, its escapist theology is anything but biblical.

Metaphorically speaking, Yahveh does approach earth's gates. Reading this psalm rightly, though, he opposes all the chaos in our world—the chaos we're so swiftly bringing on the earth too.[11] We can shut him out to our peril or we can welcome him home. But doing that means refusing the lies our world is now awash with, purifying hearts and hands.[12]

What lies? Among other things, that economic growth is an unalloyed good. That we can pillage the earth in God's name and get away with it. That living responsibly is a luxury we can't afford. That we can do to others all we least want done to us and still win our glorious King's "Well done." Refusing these lies, we open our lives to him and his salvation for both us and his world.

Prayer

Open our eyes, Lord, to the destruction we're wreaking on your good earth. Forgive our callous greed and waste and purify us, heart and hand, to live in hope. Make us bearers of your goodness, grace and glory here in the falling dark.   Amen.

25

The Secret of Life

¹For you alone I wait, Yahveh.*
²I trust in you, O my God.
Please don't humiliate me
or let my enemies revel in my ruin.
³No one who looks to you will be disgraced.
No, those who betray without cause will be disgraced.
⁴Lord, show me your paths and how to walk them.
⁵Lead me in your truth and teach me
because you're the God who saves me.
I hope in you from dawn to dusk.
⁶Remember how you've acted all through the ages—
with compassion and kindness.
⁷And forget my youthful sins* and rebellious acts.
Since you are infinitely good, Yahveh
see me only in the light of your love.

⁸Being a God of both goodness and integrity
Yahveh shows those who have gone astray
the right path to take.
⁹He leads the teachable into justice
and teaches the humble his way.

¹⁰All Yahveh's paths are marked by unfailing love
for those who keep his covenant.*
¹¹On the merits of your name, Yahveh
pardon my sin, grave as it is.
¹²What then of those who fear Yahveh?
He leads them in his chosen path
¹³they live in abundance
and their children inherit the land.
¹⁴Yahveh offers personal friendship
to those who fear him
and with it, all the wisdom of his covenant.

¹⁵My eyes are on Yahveh at all times
because he alone frees me from the traps I fall into.
¹⁶Turn to me in your grace—
I'm friendless and forlorn.
¹⁷My pain overwhelms me—
rescue me from the bind I'm in.
¹⁸Look at my weakness and affliction
and forgive all my sins.
¹⁹See how many enemies I have
and how desperately they hate me!
²⁰Rescue and protect me.
Don't humiliate me after I've sought refuge in you.
²¹I hope in you.
Let absolute integrity preserve me.
²²Redeem this Israel,* O God
from all her troubles.

Most of us in the West have a very narrow view of law. We see it as burdensome, a weight to be borne. We either carry out the law's requirements or we carry the guilt that results from not doing so. But either way, law equals burden.

Another picture we have is of law as a chain-link fence that restricts and bounds us in. Seeing endless vistas stretching out beyond the law's narrow confines, we have to make do with the dirt bare run inside the fence. So law may be safe, but its safety comes at the cost of freedom and pleasure, our supreme values.

The psalmist here holds up a third picture of law, one we seldom see in the West. She pictures a path through what we'd today call a minefield. With enemies, traps and pitfalls on every side.[1] In fact, we can't possibly make it out alive unless God shows us where to go.[2] The path the psalmist envisions demands real attentiveness[3] and discipline, but it is an exciting journey. And as we continue to look to God for help, his law leads to abundance, breadth and freedom.

The movie *An Education* (2009) pictures Jenny, a suburban London schoolgirl seduced by the gifts, freedoms and fun offered by David, a playboy nearly twice her age.[4] Making do with a brief preview of Jenny's breasts, David patiently waits till her 17th birthday to bed her amid the supposed romance of a weekend in Paris. But it's not just schoolgirls that learn the hard way. Her parents are also taken in by David's charm and the success and security he represents to them.

Not every invitation to freedom is to be taken at face value. In fact biblically speaking, only one really is—the invitation included in God's covenant. And while accepting that invitation involves discipline and attentiveness, it comes within the context of intimate personal relationship with the God of the universe. Verse 14 includes a Hebrew idiom that is literally translated "the secret of Yahveh" but which refers to mutual secret-sharing in the intimacy of personal friendship. It's not just exalted patriarchs God confides in.[5] He invites each of us to know intimacy with him.

Imitation also is at the heart of God's law. Over and over the Israelites were told that observing God's covenant was about becoming like him. He required them to consecrate themselves, but ultimately he alone could make them holy—instill his moral character in them.[6]

God wasn't merely thinking of outward conformity. Biblically understood, spirituality is having God himself painstakingly apply his law to our hearts and lives. It's not submission to a set of rules or principles, so much as to God, our friend, our heavenly lover and redeemer.

We become people of integrity by learning God's own goodness and integrity.[7] As we submit to him he teaches us what it means to be like him and empowers us to imitate his actions and grow into his very character.[8] That's why nothing is more vital on our part than humility and the willingness to be taught—what the fear of God is all about.[9]

The psalmist knows she hasn't arrived, that she doesn't deserve God's covenant blessings. And seeing herself like Israel at Sinai, she cries out as Moses did, that God will forgive her on the merits of, not her good name or character, but his.[10] She urges him to live up to his name and be the merciful and compassionate God he claims to be.

Verse 22 refers to Israel, Jacob's other name, because the psalmist identifies with Jacob, helpless and alone as the vengeful Esau and his batallion of armed men thunder down on him. And even as she begs God to rescue her, she reminds him of his commitment to redeem duplicitous sinners. God renamed Jacob "Israel" in pledge of the renovation of heart he would work in him. And so she implicitly stakes her claim in his like commitment to all who look in faith to Jacob's God.

"The secret of life is honesty and fair dealing," Groucho Marx once quipped. "If you can fake that, you've got it made." Ah, if only it was that easy! Integrity is way harder to come by and all the more so due to our inbuilt knack for faking it. That usually means relying on other gifts to camouflage our cheating—like the personal charisma David used to seduce Jenny.

Televangelists, pastors and other religious leaders can all fall back on a combination of their position, track record, personal charisma and spiritual gifts.[11] Rank-and-file believers often fall back on their religious devotion. The irreligious on other equivalent gifts and accomplishments.

The scary part of it is that we do it all so effortlessly, even while talking about transparency and integrity and loathing the hypocrisy we so plainly see in others. Dostoyevsky once remarked that "Lying to ourselves is more deeply ingrained than lying to others." That's because we're taken in by our self-directed lies—on one level at least—and use them to build something akin to an alternate reality, one that so justifies all our choices of belief and morality that we don't even see the spin we're putting on things. Such pervasive dishonesty cannot help but undermine our character, though.

And what could matter more than character? However shiny on the outside, a wormy apple is always sickening to bite into. As the hapless Jenny learns, character deficiencies eventually come back to bite us in the butt. Jenny's parents likewise fall victim to their own vanity and pretense. Integrity alone preserves us from such humiliation and ruin.

Yet what could be so impossibly beyond our grasp apart from God revealing our self-deception to us? Knowing this and that God has all the character she lacks, the psalmist hopes in his grace to her and commits to living with absolute integrity the life his covenant sets out for her.[12] That's what true spirituality is all about.

Prayer

Lord, you alone can guide me through this life and keep me honest to myself. How could I possibly be my own best guide, given my track record for self-deception? Build your integrity into my life, I pray. Make me holy in the very same way that you are holy. Not superficially, to impress others, but thoroughly that I may be whole. Forgive my sins and guide me always in your way because I put my hope in you. Amen.

27

In the Eye of the Storm

¹Yahveh* is my light and my salvation—
who should I fear?
Yahveh is my rock-solid fortress—
who is there to terrify me?
²Just as vicious thugs attack me
teeth bared for the kill
they, my enemies, trip and fall flat.
³Even when a whole army closes in on me
my heart won't give way to fear—
though war engulfs me my course remains steady.

⁴One thing I ask of Yahveh—
I long for it above all else:
to live in Yahveh's house for the rest of my life
so I can gaze on his incredible beauty
and savor his every word.
⁵For when I'm in trouble
he shelters me under his roof
grants me sanctuary in his temple
protects me beyond my enemies' reach.
⁶And when it's all over

head high, I'll fill his temple
with happy shouts and songs of praise
as I offer my thanksgiving sacrifices.

[7]So hear me, Yahveh, as I cry out to you.
Be gracious and answer me.
[8]When you said, "Seek my face"
my heart sang back:
        "Your face, Yahveh, is just what I'll seek!"
[9]Please don't hide your face from me
or turn away angrily.
You've been my help
so don't desert me now, my Savior God.
[10]Even if my mother and father disown me
Yahveh will take me in his arms.
[11]Teach me your way, Lord, and make it plain
so I don't stumble and fall into enemy hands.
[12]Please don't hand me over to them
testifying falsely against me
and threatening to destroy me.

[13]If only I could know for certain
I'd live on to see God's goodness…

[14]Wait for Yahveh to come through!
Take heart and be bold!
Wait for him to come through!

Actor Hugh Grant once said, "I don't believe in truth, I believe in style."[1] And many today see self-fulfillment in similar terms, akin to the "self-creating" freedom Michel Foucault preached. This means many things to many people, but self-stylists abhor boredom above all else. So they're often driven to keep the show going non-stop in an endless succession of original ideas, incisive analyses, outrageous quips and innovative approaches, in company with an assortment of other equally bright self-stylists.

This may work well for a while, but even the most gifted person finds having to be "on" all the time an intolerable burden. And with self as the ultimate reference point, friendship is reduced to just another means of self-fulfillment. Novelist Saul Bellow described such freedom as "bordered on all sides by isolation." However stimulating in the short term, self-styling eventually leaves us hollow, cut off from truly satisfying community.

The path the psalmist—possibly David—takes is different. So in love with God is he that everything else must find its place in relation to his supreme love. Like St. Augustine, he might describe self-fulfillment in terms of filling the God-shaped hole at the core of his being. Because he longs for Yahveh above all else, seeing him to his heart's content, discovering all his thoughts—he can't get enough of his divine lover.

With such passion, where better for him to live than in Yahveh's earthly home? Not that he actually means to camp out in his temple. But with Yahveh as his life, he can't bear to leave him, take his eyes off him or suffer the sound of his voice to be interrupted.

This involves action on his part, the heart's ready response to God's invitation to seek him[2] whether with others or alone, as here. So prayer isn't just a means to get things from God. It's asking him to reveal himself to us too. Because he is beauty itself and the center, the still point around which everything turns. Only in his revelation of himself can we truly know ourselves. Only by his light, can we find our way in this hostile world. Only centered in him do we know the sort of wholeness that holds our lives together, no matter what friends, comforts and achievements do or don't populate them at the moment. No matter what.

Of course, God seeking never takes place in a vacuum. We

find the psalmist full-flight in the middle of his life, hostile threats on every hand, false witnesses determined to bring him down. He's swimming with the sharks. By popular thinking, the dire straits he finds himself in are clear proof of his spiritual failure and so leave him very lonely. As with media exposure of a politician's or celebrity's failures today, everyone has turned on him. He fears even his parents may abandon him to the mob. So he really has nowhere else to turn but God.

Thankfully, though, Yahveh's love is the one thing that remains constant. So with his predators far too close for comfort and Yahveh not coming through when he thinks he should, he alternates between urgent requests for rescue[3] and confident statements of faith that Yahveh will rescue him.[4] Yet because Yahveh's love for him is rock-solid, because he protects him from harm and lights the way before him, the psalmist is determined to live confidently no matter what. And that gives him a remarkable sense of poise and freedom despite all his constraints.

This is the same freedom Aleksandr Solzhenitsyn discovered in the Gulag. He has the prisoner Bobynin telling his tormentor, "The man from whom you've taken everything is no longer in your power; he is free again."[5] The more the supports of his life are ripped away, the more the psalmist finds that essential freedom which is ours in God alone.

This doesn't mean we must all be so stripped down to discover God. But it is true that we discover true freedom only to the degree that we discover God, however gently or abruptly our self-seeking clutter happens to be cleared away on us. The fact that for so many religious people, finding God means anything but finding freedom only shows how easily we can be diverted from our original quest. But the psalmist won't settle for any God-substitutes. And so, despite the huge uncertainties of his life, he remains calm and concludes, urging himself and everyone else caught in this storm with him to take heart, live confidently and simply wait for

Yahveh to come.

Prayer

Seeking you, Lord, comes with no guarantee things will go as I think they should. Only the rock-solid certainty that your love will hold no matter what else gives way. So from all my misguided self-seeking, free me to seek your face. Because that vision invariably stamps your calm on me, giving me your power to move free in the eye of the storm.   Amen.

29

God of All Truth

[1]Stand back, you oversized godlings!
Stand in awe before the glory and power!
[2]Acknowledge Yahveh* as unrivalled star of the show.
Bow low before him —
perfect mystery, matchless glory!

[3]Yahveh's voice starts low
rumbling over the sea's wild roar
and crescendos into mind-numbing bursts of thunder
[4]commanding, magisterial!
[5]Yahveh's voice brings the cedars of Lebanon crashing down —
turns them into matchstick wrecks!
[6]It makes Lebanon's majestic mountains
frolic like spring calves —
Mt. Hermon wheel and gambol like a wild ox.
[7]Then it strikes terror in the liquid fire of a lightning bolt
[8]that shakes the desert right down to Kadesh!
[9]Finally, it sends the mighty oaks into a dance
so wild it strips them of their leaves.
At this point no one
in his cosmos-turned-temple can hold back

and the whole place resounds with shouts of "Glory!"

[10]Yahveh sits enthroned forever
over all the chaos of wind and waves.
[11]Giving strength to his people
he grants them his peace.

Sex and religion make a wicked marketing combo. Just ask Madonna or Dan Brown. In ancient Canaan, Ba'al worship offered that same combination with sacred sex rites for all. And given that Ba'al's divine portfolio covered rain, storms, agricultural fertility, sexual potency/fertility and victory in war, it's not surprising he was Yahveh's biggest rival. Rain was crucial and storms potentially devastating to the livelihood of agricultural Israelites living in semi-arid Palestine. And in a region famed for endless tribal warfare, the god of war was definitely someone you wanted on your side. Ba'al was said to have built his throne on the chaos of the primeval sea—meaning that he was in charge of everything. Throw in bevies of temple prostitutes, both female and male, and it's no wonder Ba'al shrines dotted the countryside everywhere.

Whenever the Israelites doubted Yahveh was really in charge or was looking out for them, they knew where to turn. Ba'al inspired not only faith, but also fear. Because with so many portfolios in his pocket, if you served Yahveh and Ba'al actually turned out to be in charge of the world, you were screwed.

So the psalmist goes toe-to-toe with Ba'al here, takes on the whole Canaanite myth. This isn't obvious to us because he never mentions Ba'al by name. But it wouldn't have escaped any of his first readers. To begin, he writes in a style that mimics Ba'al poetry, which opened with a call for all the other gods to assemble and acknowledge Ba'al's supremacy. He makes ample use of Ba'al imagery too, shows Yahveh revealing his unrivaled power and glory in a thunderstorm, of all things—even shooting down lightning bolts, Ba'al's trademark. So awesome is Yahveh's power that Ba'al and his coterie of godlings are forced to acknowledge his supremacy, which effectively un-gods them. And just in case someone still doesn't get it, the psalm ends with Yahveh permanently enthroned on the sea, the very place Ba'al's throne was said to sit. So no need to mention his name.

While Ba'al worship is no major attraction today, the psalm raises a question vital to us all. Namely, why must we choose between religions at all? Why not meld them all together like protagonist Piscine Patel does in Yann Martel's *Life of Pi*? After all, the psalmist's concern isn't just that Yahveh be admitted to the clique of Canaanite gods. He means to totally unseat Ba'al, to show him up for a mere subject of God masquerading as his Lord and to present Yahveh as the only true God.

This will seem harsh to the average pluralist today, who may not mind if you root for your religion as long as you don't knock anyone else's. Obviously, the psalm is ancient literature. But even so, what to do with it?

To begin, there's a lot to be said for the respect pluralism builds into our social discourse. We too easily grow smug in speaking with those of other faiths or no faith, as if we've nothing to learn and they nothing to teach. The reality is that we have much to learn from others. Even outright lies are only twisted truths. So how could other belief systems not have truths to teach us? And why shouldn't we embrace truth wherever we find it since all truth is God's truth? But as Wilfred Cantwell Smith observes, we typically compare our faith's ideals—how it *ought to be*—with the other faith's actual practice—how it *is*. Clearly, this apples-to-oranges approach is designed to help us dominate, rather than hear the other person out graciously and respectfully.[1]

We must be honest in our thinking and speaking, though, and honesty cuts both ways. However beautifully presented, dishonesty decomposes into a lifeless, amorphous mass. The real problem with religious intolerance isn't clarity of thought nor yet of expression. Iron—not jelly—sharpens iron.[2] The problem is that mix of dishonesty, unfairness, pride and contempt that produces bigotry. And it's no less a problem with unclear thought than clear or with pluralism than monotheism.

Western pluralism is rooted in modernity's separation of "objective facts" from "subjective beliefs and values." But the nature of reality isn't determined by popular opinion. And the basis of this dichotomy has never been established beyond the Enlightenment's determination to sideline religion and declare its own scientific knowledge supreme.

To accept $2 + 2 = 4$ rules out all other answers and the very same can be said of rape's being evil and monotheism's being true. Worshipping both Yahveh and idols is no more an option than simultaneously being both truly communist and capitalist or modernist and postmodernist. Irreconcilable differences exist between the Bible and the Bhagavad Gita. And contradictory beliefs don't work in religion any more than anywhere else. Nor does learning from each other's faith require us to consign all our beliefs and values to a cloud of unknowing. Love, justice and truth are all non-negotiables.

While there's a mystical element integral to the worship of Yahveh—since he's the subject and we always the objects of his revelation—that doesn't mean we can say nothing true about him. His self-revelation is consistently content-rich. Nor do grace and humility keep us from communicating what he's revealed of himself as faithfully and as passionately as we can.

But some will say, "Why bother? Why try to influence anyone else's understanding of God in the first place? Why not just say 'To each his own' and be done with it?" The reason is that truth really does matter and compels us to act accordingly. The praiseworthy to praise it, which is implicit throughout this psalm: no one who truly sees God in action can withhold his rightful praise.

We praise far lesser objects—rock bands, hockey teams, fine wines, etc. Mac users are notoriously passionate, even evangelistic, in their commitment to Apple computers. And the more we see our values threatened—whether by a monopolistic Microsoft, a dictatorial Hitler or a Neopagan approach to life—the more we'll want to set the record straight.

On the other hand, nothing is more annoying than contrived passion, an oxymoron if ever there was one. Poetry and evangelism expressing such limp-wristed love are the very worst kinds possible. Thankfully, this psalm is neither.

Idolatry is essentially misdirection and on a major journey even slight disorientation can be disastrous. In a day when most travel was on foot and highways non-existent, to say nothing of accurate maps and GPS devices, the psalmist would have needed no convincing there. And the Ba'al cult's misdirection was far from slight. Awed by Yahveh's greatness and love, the psalmist insists that we see him for who he is. Which is only right. In that vision, with all its holy awe, we find true life and peace.

Prayer

Why, Lord, should I trade the whole for just a part of truth or the lover of my soul for some wannabe god? So help me to love your truth even as you do and not be sidelined by bad directions. Make me no less truthful than I am humble and gracious, seeking love and wholeness where they're truly found. In you. Amen.

32

Amazing Grace

[1]How wonderful it is when your rebellion is forgiven—
whited right out of God's ledger!
[2]How enviable when Yahveh*
doesn't count your waywardness against you!
With no reason to hide
your spirit is open and artless before him.

[3]When I held all my sin* inside me
it gnawed on my bones
through the endless groan of each long day.
[4]Your discipline squeezed the life out of me day and night
sapped my strength like summer's scorching heat.
[5]Then I gave up trying to hide my sin from you
and said to myself:
    It's time to confess my rebellion to Yahveh.
So I blurted everything out
and you instantly took all the evils I'd committed away.

[6]That's why God-seekers should turn to you
before the tsunami hits.
That way the surging waters never reach them.

[7]You're my shelter, protecting me till all danger is past
filling my ears with shouts of rescue.

[8]You say:
"I'll show you the way you're to take.
All eyes, I'll teach you everything you need to know.
[9]Don't be an ass
a senseless mule that won't submit without bit and bridle
lest I use them on you."

[10]What troubles await those who rebel against you, Yahveh!
But Yahveh's constant love surrounds all who trust him.
[11]So celebrate Yahveh, all you who obey him!
Sing for joy, all you honest-hearts!

Gerald G. May renders biblical anthropology pretty succinctly when he describes human beings as "two-legged, walking, talking desires for God."[1] Sadly, Western culture has long since denied this. The majority of our leading thinkers, scientists and artists at least. Because anything that makes us in any way dependent cramps our commitment to humankind's autonomy.

But we've only to look at the desperate poverty 1.5 billion people live in, the wars splattering our planet with blood and the shocking collapse of species taking place all over the world today—from frogs, to fish, to pollinating bees, not to mention the more glorious tigers and rhinos—to see where all our vaunted autonomy takes us.

No, we were created for love and not just any love. The perfect love of God. Biblically speaking, this is the secret we all know, but often without knowing we know it. Like the alcoholic who on one level knows he has a problem, but simply can't bear the cost of facing it. So while he knows deep down, to all intents and purposes he doesn't know at all. In fact, he's usually the last to know. And all without consciously denying anything. Likewise, we submerge our knowledge of God with barely a ripple to show for it.

All the things we long for—beauty, justice, truth, love, loyalty, compassion—are really just our longings for God. Because he's the only one who answers them fully. However satisfying it may be at first, says May, every human relationship eventually disappoints us. All our other passions too, even though rewarding work and enjoyable experiences may increase their shelf life by averting our attention and helping us make do. What we don't realize is that we love all these good things "…not for themselves, but because they whisper to us of their Creator, the One we really long for."[2]

Being made in God's likeness means everything about us was designed to reflect in created terms the uncreated Lover we long for. We reflect him truly only by loving him back. So denying this longing—and we all deny it to some extent—represents the negation of all we were meant to be.

Broken as we are, we reject this Love in thought, word and deed and try to silence the voice within that tells us of our wrong. And forgetting who we are, we choose to live negatively, sometimes very destructively, and typically compound our wrong by denying what we've done or saying there's no God to offend.

Biblically, sin represents spiritual adultery, the revolt of our hearts, minds and bodies against the God we were created to love. This revolt registers in us spiritually, estranging us from God, psychologically, as sin chips away at our passion for life, and psychosomatically, as the very cells of our bodies rebel against it. The psalmist says it gnaws on his bones.[3] But intoxicated by the false logic of self-sufficiency, we hold out, foolishly refusing to admit to God the sins he already knows about.

Accepting his verdict on our sin means admitting we owe him our whole-hearted devotion 24/7. It also means accepting that we're unable to atone* for our sins. Because if we owe God 100% of our devotion every single day, how can we come up with anything more today to make up for what we cheated him of yesterday? Even if we serve him perfectly today—supposing that was possible—it would just do for today. So any idea that our good deeds annul our evil deeds is patently false. It would be like Bernard Madoff being allowed to "repay" his multi-billion dollar debt to the multitudes he swindled by simply never doing it again.

That's why the psalmist doesn't mention remorse, sacrifices or good deeds here. Because as worthy as they are in their place, they can't possibly buy forgiveness. Forgiveness is either earned or freely granted. It cannot be both.

If it's earned, this opens us up to no end of performance anxiety. Because how can we accurately determine the extent of our sins? What if we underestimate them? On the other hand, how can we accurately assess the purity of our good deeds? What if we perform them mindlessly or selfishly—what will they count for then? And what if we're short by even just 5%?

But this is all wrong. As Catholic writer Peter Kreeft says, "God is a lover. He is not a manager, businessman, accountant, owner, or puppet-master. What he wants from us first of all is not a technically correct performance but our heart."[4] And C.S. Lewis concurs, "We may think God wants actions of a certain kind, but God wants people of a certain sort."[5] He wants our love.

The only place to hide is in the God who first called Abraham to live in his mercy. Because if God had counted any of his sins against him, the whole enterprise of faith would have been doomed from the start. Forgiveness is free because God's love can't be bought or sold. Freely offered, it's ours for the taking. And its very freedom is what liberates us to love God as he first loved us. Without having to earn anything, we're freed to obey the God who loves us perfectly.

If the obedience God requires is never about paying off

our spiritual debts, what is it then? It's simply about loving God and learning to walk in his wisdom. Because surely the One who made us knows best how we should live and care for his world. Grace means that, with nothing more to hide from him, we're freed to live authentically and in our newfound honesty, to walk the path God sets before us.

That means living responsibly also. Not recklessly numbing life's pain through an endless succession of spiritual flings. It also means living joyfully. Whole-heartedly celebrating the Lover who frees us to live in his perfect love.

Prayer

How can I fathom the depths of your love for me, Lord? Though you long to lift me up to your level, my love of bootstrap salvation would reduce you to the level of my small-mindedness if it could. But your forgiveness is ours by mercy alone. So please forgive me and help me to live obediently, freely, joyfully—by your amazing grace. Amen.

42/43

Thirst

¹Like a deer pants for a rippling brook
my soul pants for you, O God!
²My whole being thirsts for the life-giving God—
when will I see his face?
³Day and night I've lived on tears
thanks to this incessant taunting:
        "Yeah, where's your God now?"
⁴I ache to think how I used to lead
pilgrim throngs to your house for sacred festivals
carried by the exuberant din of our worship…
⁵*Why are you so depressed, moaning inside?*
Hope in God!
I will yet praise him for coming to the rescue—
being my God.

⁶Depressed as I am, everywhere I go
from the Jordan trough to lofty Mount Hermon
to the last little no-name hill
I turn only to you.
⁷One churning plunge pool shouts to the next
in the roar of your waterfalls

only then for your raging rapids
to pummel and pound me and spit me out.
⁸Yet Yahveh* shows me his constant love by day
and puts his song in my heart by night—
a prayer to the God of my life.
⁹But still I ask God my Rock:
　　"Why have you abandoned me
　　left me to mourn my enemies' harassment?
　　¹⁰Their relentless taunting—'Where's your God now?'—
　　is death in my bones…"
¹¹ *Why are you so depressed, moaning inside?*
Hope in God!
I will yet praise him for coming to the rescue—
being my God.

¹Declare me innocent, O God!
Take up my cause and save me
from these faithless, lying thugs!
²You're my God, my defense.
Why have you left me to lament my enemies' harassment?
³Send out your truth and light
to lead me back to the holy hill where you live.
⁴Then I'll come before your altar—
before you, my joy and delight—
praising you on my lute, O God my God…
⁵ *Why are you so depressed, moaning inside?*
Keep on hoping in God!
I will yet praise him for coming to the rescue—
being my God.

If you've ever wondered where God was when you needed him, you'll understand these two psalms, originally one as above. The psalmist is hounded the length and breadth of the land by scoundrels bent on his ruin. Only released from one chaotic plunge pool in his freefall to the next and then made to run the whitewater gauntlet beyond, he's desperate for God.

I'd originally looked forward to writing on this psalm, one of my favorites. But as I began, a business venture I'd poured myself into for over a year was pronounced DOA, forcing me to lick my wounds and slink back onto the job search circuit. Failures in a one-man business leave little room for blame shifting. And while many would agree that selling yourself to potential employers is no treat at the best of times, it's truly farcical when you're freshly beaten up. By yourself.

You might think living the psalm would make writing about it easy. But I was raised to believe you should never be depressed, let alone admit it publicly. So spilling my guts like this didn't exactly fit my idea of what to write. But that left only one option. Waffling.

Finally after many false starts I realized my disconnect and decided that, too raw for comfort or not, I must either write honestly or forget it. Even if God still hasn't come through for me. Even if the psalmist's dark emotions, his sense of abandonment and his heartsick longing for God are still mine as I write this — along with the fear and false shame that go with admitting I feel abandoned. (Will people offer me advice I don't need or throw a party I'm not up for?)

We so often treat other people's depression as if it's not real and a good talking to or quick diversion will do the trick. But emotional pain demands as much sensitivity as physical pain. Often more. As you drag the ball and chain of your failure, real or imagined, behind you — and more likely a whole string of them — everything blends together in the dark, making perspective impossible.

You may also need to change course or think on your feet — such fun when you're feeling unsure of yourself! And with one part each of shame, confusion and self-doubt, you end up with a delightful mix of anxiety, insomnia, impulsiveness, irritability, isolation, despair—things that given enough time, lead to a million suicides a year worldwide.

When Sir Ernest Shackleton's ship *Endurance* became trapped in Antarctic pack ice, he had an even bigger task than making daily life-and-death decisions for his men. Maintaining their morale month after month, stranded amid some of earth's most inhospitable conditions.

Though solid to walk on, the 50-foot-thick pack ice was in constant motion, like earth's tectonic plates, only moving much faster. Few of his men realized their danger. But Shackleton had no illusions, confiding to his captain: "It's only a matter of time. What the ice gets, the ice keeps." Nine months later the summer thaw forced them to take what little they could carry in their lifeboats and abandon ship, moving out onto the ice floes that had crushed it.

That was when things got truly harrowing. And when their tale was finally told, they owed their survival, humanly speaking, to Shackleton's amazing ability to maintain hope. The ship Belgica had suffered the same fate a few years earlier and some of its crew "went mad."

Truth is, our mental health isn't as solid as we imagine. We're better to think of it like Antarctic pack ice, with one relatively solid floe colliding with another and a mental "break-up" being just a matter of having the right conditions. Our external threats are only half the battle and the clearer we see that, the stronger we are to fight on both fronts.

But the internal front is what makes depression so very lonely. No matter how supportive family and friends are—mine surely have been—who can really understand what you alone feel? Many people are either blamed or shunned for their illness—and what I say about depression is far worse with schizophrenia and other more debilitating mental illnesses. Nor do you want to drag others down with you.

Even if friends and family offer much needed support, who better to lead you home than the God who knows your inmost thoughts and loves you still? So the psalmist asks God to send out his truth and light, like the pillar of cloud and fire that led the Israelites to the Promised Land. He then staves off despair by repeated rounds of prayer and self-talk and by nurturing his longing for God. Three times he questions his mental approach and three times tells himself to hope in God.

And he recalls what Zion* means.[1] It means God present in his world to welcome, bless and defend from evil. It means community, with all the richness of belonging, a shared cause, mutual support and gifts used for the good of all—one of his being leadership. And it means worship, the holy celebration of God's faithfulness in joyful song.

So the psalmist protests his enemies' taunts, laments his lonely exile, asks God why he hasn't shown up and begs him to vindicate and lead him home. But most of all, he commits to continue praising him for coming through for him. And he does that in advance. Repeating the words by faith till he feels as well as knows they're true.[2]

Prayer

With failures and losses chasing me down a desert canyon, I thirst for you, Lord! Why are the taunts of my one-time friends still unanswerable? Come to my rescue, light my way and lead me home to you. Because I'm determined to hope in you till you do and everyone sees that you're my God. Amen.

46

A Tale of Two Cities

¹God is our refuge, our stronghold
always there for us when we're in trouble.
²So we won't fear
even when the earth quakes
and its mountains come crashing down into the sea.
³Though its waters rage
and their battering shakes the mountains.

⁴Brimful of joy
a river streams through God's city
holy residence of the Most High.
⁵With God living here—
defending his home as dawn breaks—
it will not fall.
⁶Superpowers rant and superpowers rot.
When he speaks the earth dissolves.
⁷Yahveh,* Commander of heaven's armies, is for us.
Jacob's God is our fortress.

⁸Come, see what Yahveh has done
the devastation he's wreaked on earth:

[9]breaking bows, snapping spears in two
and burning chariots to ashes
he's banned war everywhere on the planet.
[10]"Give up! Admit I'm God!" he cries.
"Supreme over the superpowers
supreme over all the earth!"
[11]Yahveh, Commander of heaven's armies, is for us.
Jacob's God is our fortress.

Many today decry the violence of the Torah* and of the Psalms in particular. While I appreciate their concerns, I'd urge them to look beyond religion's modern-day champions whose cockeyed dreams of the New Jerusalem make the earth a mere throwaway, who build military arsenals capable of destroying life on a massive scale or expropriate Palestinian land only to build massive walls across it, degrading and dehumanizing both captive and captor.

Little wonder Muslim unrest festers in our world like an open sore. But all this violence relates to a very different Zion* from the one spoken of here. Because while this psalm has much to say about violence, its real subject is the God of all peace.[1]

My point is that the callous attitudes, rampant environmental abuse—what Tracy Chapman calls "the rape of the world"—and self-serving militarism the Torah appears to inspire in so many are all based on misreadings of the text. In effect, before pillaging the earth and each other, we pillage the Good Book for whatever pretexts we can find and so fashion God into a small-g "god" who holds all our opinions and rubber-stamps all we do.

But can the psalmist be against militarism when she calls Yahveh the "Commander of heaven's armies"? Yes, she begins with the world we live in, a world filled with devastation, natural, political and military. But she isn't afraid because she's found shelter in none other than Jacob's God, Commander of heaven's armies. Rooted in Israel's* definitive salvation stories, those phrases tell us what kind of general Yahveh is.

The first takes us back to the night Jacob hears that Esau, the brother he cheated so long before, is advancing against him with an army of 400 men. With Jacob's bag of tricks completely empty, he can already imagine the carnage as his brother slaughters his whole family before his eyes. But that's when he encounters God and, latching onto him, refuses to let go unless God grants him his blessing. An all-out, night-long brawl ensues. Finally as dawn breaks, God simultaneously puts Jacob's hip out of joint and blesses him. So while he appears more vulnerable than ever, hobbling toward his brother for the dreaded meeting, he actually has a newfound confidence—not in himself, but in the One who is his shelter and his God.[2]

The second phrase, "Commander of heaven's armies," takes us back to the night Moses leads the Israelites across the sea with Pharaoh in hot pursuit. Again God's people are desperate—lost without him. And again he comes through for them at the break of dawn, closing the waters of the sea on Pharaoh and his superpower army.[3]

This God, who is bigger than politics, bigger than superpowers, bigger than creation itself, is on Israel's side. So why should God's people fear? Living among them in Zion, Yahveh will once again come through for them at the break of dawn.

Accounts of the Assyrian siege of Jerusalem, which this psalm is so suggestive of, bear this out. Power-hungry Sennacherib of Assyria, the superpower of the day, sends a massive army to besiege little Jerusalem. King Hezekiah promptly sends out his negotiators. But the Assyrian general proceeds to trash the negotiations by shouting his propaganda to the Israelite soldiers looking on from the city walls. Brazenly boastful, he alternately mocks the "hicktown" Yahveh and claims it was as-a-matter-of-fact Yahveh who authorized his attack.

Demoralized and desperate, Hezekiah turns to God. And

replying through his prophet, God says all the general's rants will come to nothing since he himself will defend his city. Which is exactly what happens. The big shot general rushes off to handle a crisis on another battlefield and the very next day the city wakes up to find that a plague has decimated the entire Assyrian camp.[4]

What does this say to us today, more the perpetrators than the victims of devastation, back of which stands our rampant consumerism? Despite all our celebrated technological advances, we humans are "...challenged more than ever before to demonstrate our mastery—not over nature but of ourselves." So said Rachel Carson, author of *Silent Spring.*[5]

And how often it is women who hold us men to account in our dealings with nature. Honored with a Nobel prize for opposing an oppressive regime and founding a movement to reforest Kenya's defoliated lands, environmentalist Wangari Maathai is another woman who has spoken out with prophetic urgency. When will we take Mother Earth's needs seriously?

We also wreak devastation upon each other. Lamenting the international loan sharks' use of insupportable debt to turn entire nations in the Developing World into glorified labor camps, Bruce Cockburn once described the IMF as "modern slavers in drag as champions of freedom."[6] Since the early 80's, British rocker Bob Geldof, U2's Bono and a host of others in the ONE Campaign have made significant gains against this travesty of justice. But still today millions die of hunger in a world of plenty simply because so many of us are blissfully ignorant of the economic atrocities our democratic silence makes us party to.

I must mention one last area of devastation here. Sadly, our advanced use of technology reaches its pitch in a playroom full of military toys that include germ warfare, chemical warfare— things like napalm and Agent Orange—smart bombs, dirty bombs, uranium-depleted cluster bombs, nuclear bombs and neutron bombs. What kind of human greatness is it that's exercised most brilliantly in its inhumanity? And what kind of world order can we hope to build through hate and fear?

Against all our devastation, God here proposes a radical alternative to a world so bent on its own twisted autonomy. That we grant him his rightful place as King. After all, he's the only licensed global policeman in the house. Only surrendered to his lordship, can we know true peace, joy and wholeness—as individuals and nations both.

But such submission actually represents our buying into *his* future far more than his promising to insure *ours.* That should be clear from the way the psalmist revels not only in God's ending this particular military campaign, but also in his banishing war universally. She looks forward to an event far more decisive than the one she's just witnessed.[7] Being of that magnitude, it would have to include the removal of all of war's precursors too. So what it really spells is the end of all our ruthless business practice, abusive violence and injustice in God's great victory over evil forever. Hallelujah!

Prayer

Forgive us, Lord, for forgetting we're not God. For living in fear, which only breeds aggression. Renouncing all our dirty deals, our dirty bombs and all the greed and fear behind them, we give up, Lord! Teach us your wisdom, joy and peace. Reign over all the earth, I pray, starting right here with me! Amen.

51

Sinners Made New

[1]Have mercy on me, O God, in your unfailing love.
Blot out my offenses in the overflow of your mercy
[2]Wash away my sin* and cleanse me of evil.
[3]Because my crimes I know well—
they haunt me night and day.
[4]Against you and you only have I sinned
doing what you clearly marked out as evil.
So your charge against me is right and your verdict just.

[5]I'm a born rebel, Lord, born to rebels as I was.
[6]And you demand truth even where no one else can see.
So teach me your wisdom in my heart of hearts.
[7]Cleanse me with hyssop[a] and I'll be pure.
Wash me whiter than snow.
[8]Fill me with such laughter and song
that the bones you've crushed jump for joy.
[9]Look past my sins and wipe away my guilt.
[10]Give me a brand new heart, O God
one that beats with pure and faithful love.

---

[a] Oregano, a plant used in ritual purification

[11]Don't throw me out of your presence
or withdraw your holy spirit from me.
[12]Restore to me the joy of your salvation
and make my heart once again long to obey you.

[13]Then I'll tell my fellow rebels about your grace
and they'll come running back to you.
[14]Wash this blood off my hands, O God, my savior!
Save me and I'll sing for joy over your forgiveness.
[15]Unstop my mouth, Lord
and I'll tell everyone what you've done.

[16]It's not sacrifices* you want from me.
No, burnt-offerings can't satisfy you.
[17]The only sacrifice you accept is a humble heart.
The soul whose only hope is you, you never reject, O God.

[18]Bless Zion* and help her—
rebuild her walls.
[19]Then you'll smile on the sacrifices we humbly bring
both big and small
and we'll offer young bulls on your altar again.

Sin is a nasty and perverse subject by any estimate. So bothersome
that we barely mention it nowadays except to market goods or
elicit the odd laugh on late night talk shows.

What makes it so onerous? Three things come to mind,
problems that hold true whether we're talking murder and adultery
or common pride and greed.

The first problem is that sin makes us such ready targets for
scorn and abuse, something we all—religious people especially—
excel in heaping. This heightens the sinner's sense of guilt and
shame. So defensively, automatically even, that she may deny the

God she sees behind it or else simply the wrong in what she's done. But either way, she cuts herself off from God's grace, the only remedy for her gracelessness.

This scorn and abuse derives from an us-them split which externalizes sin in others. But we've all rebelled against God. So as comforting as it is, that divide doesn't actually exist. Still we falsely connect its scorn with God's absolute intolerance of evil and its abuse with his white-hot judgment.

Human scorn and abuse only parody God's responses, though. Because at the heart of our scorn is contempt for others, while God's rejection of evil moves in the exact opposite direction. Its concern is the sinner's inherent dignity and worth. But we who profess biblical faith can hardly blame outsiders for this confusion when we so often model it ourselves.

The second problem is that sin leaves us so thoroughly conflicted of heart. On one level, we know adultery, for example, is dishonorable. Yet in our brokenness we're drawn to it like a moth to flame. And using all our creativity to make sin look reasonable, right and good, we become fools.

Closely related to this is the fact that the sins we see so clearly in others we're usually blind to in ourselves. Maybe not the first time we cross a given line. But little by little our charms work their magic on us till we see what we want and no more.

One man says his adultery doesn't violate his marriage because he and his wife no longer love each other—so what's to violate? He feels it's fine so long as a) it enables him to function in a loveless marriage for his kids' sake and b) he genuinely loves his lover.

Another man decides his adultery isn't wrong precisely because he *doesn't* love the call girls he visits. Too overworked and stressed to perform sexually with his wife, he convinces himself that frequenting prostitutes frees him to love his wife in other ways.

A third man turns cynic, insisting that it's cheat or be cheated

FAITHSONGS

on since "Everybody cheats!" That it hurts nobody as long as nobody knows. That the drive he succumbs to is normal and natural. That having sex is really no big deal and, anyways, monogamy is a stupid idea since no relationship can sustain its passion forever...

There's no end to our ingenuity here. Yet it's all spent on something that, however adrenaline-pumping wild, deadens us inside since it cuts us off from both Truth and Love.

But can't adultery or any other sin be loving? Yes, but only in a me-centered universe. Everywhere else it involves love repudiating love. Everywhere else it describes a relational horror we would wish on no one, but a horror that is sadly home to millions of people.

While religious people certainly have no monopoly on morality, it's also true that highly principled people, people who care deeply about justice in a million other ways often violate it at the one point that matters most: giving God the love and obedience he's due. And all the more so when our culture so typically deprecates such things as faithfulness, loyalty and obedience. But our sin is always first and foremost against the God who is love.

This leads inevitably to the third problem, that our sin makes us our own worst enemy, wreaking havoc in us the psalmist likens to crushed and broken bones, hopeless apart from God. We're all willing to admit we've messed up at times. But admitting we're so messed up that only God can save us from ourselves is no easier for us garden-variety sinners than it is for alcoholics or drug addicts.

Pogo had it right, "...we have met the enemy and he is us."[1] But today's cafeteria-style approach to spirituality makes admitting the extent of our brokenness all too easy to sidestep. Still, if an earthquake leaves your home needing massive repairs, how could anything warrant denying that fact? And the Tanakh plainly asserts—as does the New Testament after it—that apart from God we're all lost sinners.[2]

But if it's no good wishing sin away, it's equally true that diagnosis isn't cure. It only points to it. So having rejected rationalization, acknowledged that his sin is primarily against God and recognized his need of authenticity, the psalmist cries out for God's mercy, his only hope. Mercy that not only cleanses his sin, but also restores his dignity, purpose, direction, wholeness and joy—that gives him back his life.

We can all imagine some halfway forgiveness that leaves sinners second-rate, branded for life—where they're allowed back at the table provided they say nothing during the meal. But the psalmist will have none of it. He knows of a grace that makes sinners new and tunes their hearts to sing its praise. Far from making us second-rate believers, this grace makes us all its spokespersons. This is the good news that's vital to God's take on sin: however great our sin is, his grace is greater still.

Grace isn't earned through sacrifice or good deeds. It's ours only as God's free gift. And there's a wonderful leveling in that because none of us can offer anything to God except as we're renewed by his grace. Seeing that, we come with broken hearts and humbly embrace his forgiveness. His grace is what makes us pure and steadfast in love. His grace is what frees us to give our sacrifices and ourselves to him. Only by his grace can we offer God the obedience he requires.

Prayer

Virus-like, sin takes heart and mind together, Lord, dealing its double death to me. Only in your searing truth is there grace and release. So now humble my heart to hear you, forgive my sins and make me new. Grant me your grace and by it your freedom, fullness and joy, I pray. Amen.

62

Life on the Edge

[1]Only in God does my soul find rest—
in God who saves me.
[2]He alone is my Rock, my deliverance
my fortress where nothing can shake me.

[3]How long do you attack a man
all of you determined to batter him to the ground—
this leaning wall, this buckling bulwark?

[4]They've determined to knock him down
from his lofty position.
They delight in deception—
outwardly blessing, inwardly bashing.
[5]*Find rest, my soul, in God alone!*
He's the one I hope in.
[6]*He alone is my Rock, my deliverance*
my fortress where nothing can shake me.
[7]God is the one who restores my honor.
I'm rock-solid secure in him.
[8]Everyone, trust in him always.
Pour out your heart to God

because he really is our refuge.
⁹The poor are just a breath—
the rich and powerful emptiness.
Put them both on the balance
and together they add up to nothing.
Just airy breath.
¹⁰Don't trust in oppression.
Don't bankrupt your soul through extortion.
No matter how much money it promises
don't set your heart on it.

¹¹Here's what God has said—
two things we can be sure of:
God is the measure of strength
¹²and you, Yahweh,* are unfailing love.
You will certainly reward each of us
for everything we've done.

Vancouver has often been recognized as one of the world's best places to live. And its reputation was enhanced by its playing host to the 2010 Winter Olympics, with all the glowing media images that garners.

But there's a dark side to Vancouver too, a side most politicians here would rather forget. Just blocks from the site of the city's gleaming Olympic venues, its Downtown Eastside (DTES) is in many ways a world away.

Home to the city's visible sex trade, this is Canada's worst slum. Here rough sleepers cuddle concrete, malnourished people fill soup kitchens, wasted addicts transact desperate back-alley deals, binners with carts loaded high line up outside bottle depots. It's easier for under-aged teenagers to buy pot, heroin and crack than cigarettes. And with needle sharing prevalent, the DTES was not long ago said to have the highest rate of HIV infection of any neighborhood in North America.[1]

To each of the neighborhood's homeless people, the government presently gives a whopping $210 a month. Nearly ¾ of that will go to keeping them in cigarettes—at black market prices too. And over half the neighborhood's 16,000 housed residents are just a rung or two up from homelessness—many living in the squalor of vermin-infested single room occupancy buildings (SROs). Often in windowless rooms.

In its rush to clean up the neighborhood for the 2010 Olympics, the city demolished a number of SROs, evicting all residents. That included the hundreds of rats inhabiting each building, rats that should have been exterminated. So rats flooded into the streets seeking homes elsewhere and shocking visitors by their numbers and the boldness of their nocturnal foraging.

Who chooses to live in a neighborhood like this? People live here for many different reasons. Some just live here in transit. Some have lived here their whole lives, grew up here and see it as home. Some have moved into the neighborhood because they're committed to seeing it renewed. Others have come for a trendy loft apartment cheaper than anywhere else this close to work.

But many who live here don't feel they have a whole lot of choice. Over half of DTES residents are mentally ill. And the government played a pivotal role in making that demographic a reality when it closed virtually all institutions for the mentally ill back in the 80's.

To the politicians involved, it was an irresistible money-saving bid. But biblically speaking, bankrolling your future on the backs of society's poorest members is called oppression. And in a democracy we're all culpable for that. [2]

Already poor, stigmatized for their illness and on mind-altering drugs—albeit prescribed ones—most discharged patients wound up in the DTES. They met less stigma here than elsewhere and could easily mingle their prescription drugs with the street drugs so readily available. Now 20 years later the government admits they made a mistake but has done little to right it.

Who else chooses to live in the DTES? Many residents are victims of foster home abuse, physical, emotional or sexual. Many are native aboriginals—some of them survivors of residential church schools, but all victims of Canada's "Indian Act." Many DTES residents are of Chinese descent, their families having long suffered racial profiling. And regardless of your racial origins, if you've bought into whatever lies people have told you about yourself, there are real advantages to living in a ghetto where you can just disappear.

Many DTES residents have an exemplary work ethic, are very steady and industrious, even if some of them have never had a legal job in their entire lives. Others, for one reason or another, have had numerous jobs but never held any for long.

The problems of Vancouver's DTES are admittedly highly complex. So much so that most politicians don't believe change is possible. They just throw up their hands and say, "Why throw money into a black hole?" And what's true of Vancouver is to varying degrees true of most big cities and even spills over into many of their suburban areas. It's also true of our global village as a whole. Many of the world's most economically depressed nations battle the highest incidence of malnutrition and HIV/AIDS,[3] even as rich Western nations grind them down through crippling international cartels and loan payments.

The psalmist here speaks of the temptation to oppress and exploit the most vulnerable. And many of us will be shocked to think we've ever succumbed to it. But of course, we have. In a multiplicity of ways—most of them quite legal.

Legal exploitation takes place though government policies like the one that closed Vancouver's mental health institutions. It happens through governments that bankroll their success by robbing foster children, the elderly or otherwise marginalized of care they so desperately need.

Exploitation happens in our global village and implicates us all in many ways. In American Saipan's sweatshops[4] and South Africa's gold mines. Through the IMF and World Bank too. Making something legal doesn't make it moral.

The cutthroat aggression of the evildoers the psalmist has in mind makes them prey on the weak and vulnerable. People who—though made in God's image—are "leaning walls," barely hanging on.[5]

But obtaining wealth by gouging others impoverishes our souls.[6] The same money that represents God's rich blessing when obtained through hard work and good stewardship is a curse when obtained through exploitation and oppression. So however tempting such ill-gotten gain is, we'll avoid it like the plague if we value our souls.

I once worked for a prominent Christian businessman whose employees hated him for his exploitation and stinginess—and there's really no clear line between those two. All of it was cloaked in suave salesmanship,[7] making it more bearable in one sense and more galling in another. But economic necessity kept most of his employees from voicing their anger too loudly. And when the "big man" visited our office, everyone scurried around trying desperately to please him—as if they actually loved him.

Regardless, the vaunted power of such individuals amounts to nothing in the end. The psalmist's point in verse 9 is not that human beings have no value in God's eyes. It's that we've got it all wrong if we think the wealthy are any more important than the poor. As God measures us, the rich and powerful carry no more weight than the marginalized.

So partnering with rich oppressors—as do governments the world over *regardless of the political system in play*—represents a major miscalculation, however attractive it is. Because make no mistake, God will ultimately pay oppressors back for all they've taken from the poor of both material and immaterial wealth—things like honor, dignity and place.[8]

Fighting for social and global reform is absolutely vital. But even doing that, we must remember that ultimately God is our only refuge.

That resonates with many of Vancouver's DTES residents who look to God for rescue and restoration. So the psalmist urges us to trust God and pour out our hearts to him. No matter how bad things get, he's our unshakeable fortress, our refuge, our rest.[9]

Prayer

How easily impressed I am by the rich—many of whom have bought their wealth and power through oppression, at the cost of their souls. Steel my heart to extortion's siren song, Lord. Help me believe all the power really is yours. That you're the one who grants true safety, honor and rest. Help me to trust you and, like you, to side with the poor.   Amen.

65

Between Friends

¹All praise belongs to you, O God, in Zion*
and with it the keeping of vows.
²All humankind comes to you, the hearer of prayers.
³Though our sins* overwhelm us
you atone* for them all.
⁴How lucky the woman, the man
you invite to live in your presence!
At home in your holy temple—your home—
we're overwhelmed by your goodness.

⁵As the God who saves us
you answer our prayers with awesome acts
⁶which make you the hope of everyone on earth.
Clothed with the power that fixed the mountains in place
⁷you still the uproar of nations
no less than the sea's wild roar
the thunder of its crashing waves.
⁸Even earth's most distant peoples
stand in awe of your greatness
as sunrise and sunset respond with joy.
⁹You care for the earth, water it and make it fertile.

Cascading down to earth, O God
your rain-rivers never run dry
and nurture earth's crops by your design.
[10]You soak each ridge and furrow
melt them into one
and make seedlings spring up under your blessing.
[11]You crown the year with your goodness
as everything you touch overflows with your bounty.
[12]Wastelands turn into rich pastures
while the hills dress up in their party best.
[13]The pastures are clothed with flocks
the valleys garbed in golden grain.
They all sing and shout for joy!

Biblically understood, prayer is dialog, conversation with God. Friendship in fact.[1] Contrary to popular thinking, it's not about always being "proper" or "nice." It's about being real with God. Pretended niceness minimizes real relationship and robs prayer of its very best help.

But many don't see this. In fact, there are two popular spiritual alternatives to biblical prayer.[2] The first seeks something akin to remote control, with prayer as ritual performance and the God/god addressed being distant, engaging with us in only formal transactions. Words and postures are often prescribed here, as is behavioral style—generally either extreme politeness or emotionalism or some combination of the two. Repetition is usually a key factor also.

The other popular spiritual alternative views faith as a kind of power tapping. Here we obtain what we want by means of charms and sacred objects or materials. Or by engaging in positive mental imaging or prosperity consciousness via the law of attraction.[3] Either way, we "tap into" the powers that be—whether a god/God or the Universe—and use him/her/it for our ends.

As different as these two alternatives are, many combine them. Both treat prayer as a technique for getting what we want, not for getting to know and understand God's heart for us. And both typically guarantee results, provided we've got the technique down and perform it to the required extent.

Many who combine them today embrace New Age spirituality, which is all about mix-n-match. In fact the New Age offers a bewildering array of supernatural beings—a downsized "God," gods, angels, faeries, Ascended Masters and everything in between. While horoscope writers, fortunetellers, mediums and personal energy consultants bring guidance akin to God's Word, it's left up to you to decide which particular word(s) to lay hold of through positive imaging or prosperity consciousness. And you can bolster your faith through a vast catalog of supports—everything from meditation and prayer wheels to energy crystals, magic and shamanism.

But open-ended choice is the New Age's weakness far more than its strength.[4] So vast a range of configurations melds into a shapeless blur, especially grounded in nothing more than your ever-changing consciousness. So accommodating is it that it leaves no room for a God who loves us passionately and seeks all our love in return. That leaves the New Age with no God you'd want to be in constant communion with. And making things up as you go along invariably leads to a muddle of truth and error.

Many Christians, Muslims and Jews combine ritual prayer with prosperity consciousness too. Ritual plays a significant role in biblical prayer and we're sometimes called to believe God for the "impossible." But whenever we believe our prayers or faith *merit* the answers we seek, we reduce prayer to tokens for the ultimate vending machine—God. Positive imaging has its place too. But to equate faith with positive imaging makes it a form of manipulation, which neither Bible nor Qur'an ever shows God to be open to.

The psalms certainly have their ritual value, not to mention their psychological value in reorienting us to the God who blesses us. But the entire point of biblical religion and the larger context of the psalms is personal relationship with God. The psalmists wrote not so we could remember what it was like for *them* so much as to let it guide and inform us in *our* relationship with God.

But many can't see the forest for the trees. We forget healthy religion isn't mainly about getting stuff from God—whether assurance of salvation or anything else. Nor about currying God's favor with our undivided attention. It's about loving him and allowing him to remake us into something more real than we can now imagine.

One of biblical religion's cleverest counterfeits is that evangelical Christian version of it that talks endlessly about friendship with God but always within a context of niceness and the sort of polite unreality that circumvents real relationship. It often sounds and even looks like friendship with God. But its essential unreality draws it irresistibly towards one or the other of biblical prayer's spiritual alternatives, if it prays at all. Thanks to our Western "doctrine of niceness," this unreality threatens all North American evangelicals, calling for constant watchfulness.[5]

Healthy love relationships grow in at least three dimensions. In understanding the other person, even as we grow in self-awareness. In appreciating the other person, as we grow in self-appreciation. And in commitment to the other person, as we grow in self-commitment—e.g. in terms of healthy boundaries. If conversation is the primary means for growing in relationship, then honest prayer is the primary means for getting to know God.

God responds to our cries forgiveness by atoning for our sins[6] and without that we have no relationship with him. Thankfully he welcomes repentant sinners home and never remotely withholds his best from them either.[7] God answers our other prayers too, however big or small.[8] But he does so as our friend, not some remote intergalactic official.

What we do when our lives go sideways, whether in large measure or small, is critical. We choose a life of either blasphemy—railing against God—or honest prayer. Interestingly, blasphemy fits quite well with both remote-control prayers and power-tapping faith, provided we keep it separate from them. What blasphemy doesn't work with is prayer as friendship with God— the kind that makes us more real, more human, more ourselves.[9]

God is so gloriously real, says Huston Smith, you'd expect us to be drawn to his reality like iron filings to a magnet. But with so much unreality in us—so much that's not attracted to God—it's not quite that simple.[10] Since true prayer is drawing near to God, we must often begin by asking him for a heart to seek him.

Finally, God answers our prayers for regular, ordinary things like daily bread. Which leads us to celebrate his generous care for us. In agricultural Palestine's semi-arid climate, the coming of rain was critical. So the psalmist concludes by celebrating the rain and sunshine God so bountifully sends to bless the earth and fill it with joy.[11]

Prayer

Thank-you for listening to me and atoning for my sins, for your friendship and blessing, God. Don't let me settle for counterfeits of that prayer that leads to joyful, unfettered reality. Help me abandon my blasphemy for honest, humble prayer. Forgive me and draw me close to you, Lord.   Amen.

76

Perfect Hero

[1]God is celebrated in Israel*
his greatness known to one and all.
[2-3]He lives in Jerusalem and calls Zion* —
where he shattered the flaming arrow
sword and shield—his home.

[4-5]You are spectacular, God!
Magnificent on the mountains
where you plundered their champions!
They couldn't wake up—
couldn't lift a finger, God of Jacob
[6]when your blast
stopped all their horses and chariots dead.

[7]You are to be revered.
Who can stand up to you when you're angry?
[8]You pronounced your judgment from heaven
and the earth sat in stunned silence
[9]when you stood up, O God
to make things right on earth and rescue all the oppressed.
[10]Even human rage attests to your greatness

as you respond with the very least of your fury.
[11]So make vows to Yahveh, your God, and keep them.
Everyone bring tribute to the awesome One
[12]who curbs the blind ambition of kings and generals
leaving them in awe before him.

Bob Dylan once said that what makes you a hero is understanding the responsibility that goes with your freedom. I think the psalmist could work with Dylan's definition. Because not only does she picture Yahveh as having ultimate power and freedom, but also as someone who uses it to the maximum good.

God's heroism is marked by three things. First, Yahveh is compassionate. He truly cares for the downtrodden poor and uses his great power to rescue them. By contrast, Alexander, Caesar and Napoleon each represent the standard male hero whose ambition (read: ego) keeps him from caring too much about others. Yahveh is above all such petty, short-lived striving. He has nothing to prove. All power is his already.

We may not know that. We may defiantly rage against him. But he incorporates into his plans even our worst attempts to thwart him.[1] So that even our most furious attacks on God only end up making us look smaller and him bigger. In that sense, all our fist shaking keeps time to his music. And with nothing at all to prove, he's free to act on behalf of others—the weak and the disenfranchised—bringing their abuse to an end.

Second, the psalmist presents Yahveh as a humble hero. Great king of the universe that he is, he chooses to live among his people in Jerusalem. And the Torah* is at great pains to reveal the decidedly sketchy beginnings of the Israelites. Abraham and Jacob in particular fail miserably. The point being that God doesn't choose them for *their* goodness or greatness but rather to reveal *his* goodness and greatness in reaching down to them. And likewise, though there are many more glorious locations for his imperial city, he chooses Zion partly because of the kind of victory it represents in the apparently impossible overthrow of evil.

Heroism and humility don't often go together. Alexander, Caesar and Napoleon consistently strove to maximize their own glory. Yahveh doesn't need to do that because all the glory is his too. Heroism and humility are inseparable in God. Great as he is, he's not afraid to look weak or humble. Many are surprised to hear of humility in God. But the Tanakh's* most basic moral principle is that we should model our lives after God's character. And Micah 6:8 spells out his character for us in terms of justice, compassion and humility.

Third, Yahveh is a just hero. He's the warrior-king who makes things right on the earth, rescuing the oppressed and balancing the ledger. Seldom as fast as we'd like. But still he's unwaveringly committed to making things right on the earth, cutting earth's tyrants down to size and destroying all the weapons of war.

The psalmist doesn't give enough detail for us to be sure which story she has in mind. It could be the one I told in chapter 46, of Yahveh's triumph over the Assyrians in 2 Kings 19. Isaiah prophesied the Assyrians' defeat and by the very next morning their entire army had been decimated by a deadly epidemic—rendered unable to lift their weapons or even wake up. And God had barely glanced their way.

Many people have problems with this psalm. Some are disturbed by the idea that God is biased in favor of the poor. But that bias runs through the Tanakh from beginning to end. If this disturbs us, it puts us on the side of those who oppress the poor.[2]

Others react to the psalm's strong military motif and still others to the very thought of God's "interfering" to right wrongs. They see an impersonal law of karma—that the universe is *automatically* set up to reward our good and bad deeds in kind—as far less problematic. This is largely because any idea of a personal God overseeing the process flies full in the face of our culture's first article of faith, our "doctrine of niceness." That doctrine makes God only permissible insofar as he's nice, effectively leaving no room for his justice. And who wants an unjust God? So we get rid of God rather than rethink our notion of niceness.

If we trash God for the sake of niceness, we're left with a number of popular alternatives. We can embrace nihilistic chaos or we can forfeit all real personality—God's and our own too—in, say, Buddhism. These represent avant-garde and ancient-exotic choices respectively, each with its own appeal. Alternatively, we may redefine God as whatever else appeals to us in some sort of New Age concoction or else merely float, uncommitted to any one view but still carried by our culture's strong current of anti-traditionalism.

The good thing about all these choices is that they appeal to people sick and tired of the falsehood, egotism and warmongering of so many Christians, Muslims and Jews. They represent a kind of escape, which always seems easier. But ultimately neither our rootless amorality, our do-it-yourself religion, our feel-good psychobabble nor our mindless floating turns out to be any easier than God.

Granted, the psalmist doesn't make things easy either. But since when was easy the final test of truth? Ultimately we aren't given a choice as to the nature of reality. We either face it—own it—or else try to evade it.[3]

To me, this leaves us no choice but to radically rethink our false expectations of God and why we find the psalmist's concept of justice so bothersome. Do we fear that the axe of God's judgment threatens the roots of our tree? And if so, how might that influence our thinking?

We need rather to recall the last verse of the second psalm. Why expend all our energy trying to evade reality? The autonomy we're so desperate for is the very thing that's killing us. On the other hand, if we surrender to God, we'll find that "all that awaits us is blessing."

Answering to all that we are, the heroism the psalmist proclaims has the ring of truth to it, which even the blather of our most bloated religious leaders can't drown out. That tells me I've not chosen it so much as it's chosen me. And for that, I'm eternally grateful.

Prayer

Lord, you call me to be the kind of hero you are. Bold and courageous, yet humble, just and compassionate. That's an order I can't begin to fill unless you live in me. But what else is the freedom you've given me for? So help me to shun every alternative and embrace you as my perfect hero!   Amen.

87

City of God

[1]He founded it on the holy mountain
[2]and Yahveh* loves Zion*
more than all the cities of Israel.*

[3]What incredible things are said of you, city of God:
    [4]"I'll register Egypt and Babylon
    among those who know me.
    Palestine, Lebanon and Nubia too—
    all 'Nativeborn Citizens.'"

[5]And of Zion they'll say:
    "Imagine, people from every nation under heaven
    all full citizens!"

The Most High himself
will bring his city to its fulfillment.
[6]Yahveh will register earth's peoples
as all equally his own.

[7]Then they'll celebrate with song and dance, saying:
    "All my wellsprings are in you!"

Nothing pulls more powerfully on the world's monotheistic faiths today than pluralism. Nothing, that is, but fundamentalism, which fundamentalists in all three faiths see as the vital antidote to pluralism. And fundamentalism is a huge factor in the so-called clash of civilizations.

The 2001 destruction of the ancient Buddhas of Bamyan was largely a Taliban "giving of the finger" to Western pluralists. The abusive picketing, lawsuits and spittle of Topeka's antigay Westboro Baptist Church and the threatened Qur'an burning of Gainesville's Terry Jones are its Christian equivalents. So hostile are such anti-pluralists that they often seem to take a grim satisfaction in being hated by their enemies.

But besides eliciting strong reactions, pluralism evokes attractive religious accommodations also, as Jewish, Christian and Muslim leaders produce versions of "monotheistic pluralism" embraced by many. The problem is that by definition monotheism isn't open to pluralism's basic idea—namely, that "all roads lead to the top of the mountain." Instead it insists that the one true God has spoken and everyone must heed his words.

Monotheism shares many truths with other religions and some of pluralism's key values also. But it draws a line when it comes to the equal validity of contradictory truth systems. To cross that line invariably yields something like Hinduism's acceptance of God, which however well-intended, renders him just one god among millions, distinguished only by his Jewish, Christian or Muslim storyline and accessories. In fact, God's peerlessness is the *sine qua non* of monotheism. Putting a capital G on the word is irrelevant if you make idolatry okay—even just for others—or God's plan of salvation just one among many.

While the more liberal monotheist's cohabitation with pluralism is by now passé, pluralistic liaisons by more orthodox monotheists still raise eyebrows. *The Dignity of Difference: How to Avoid the Clash of Civilizations* by Chief Rabbi Sir Jonathan

Sachs offers a highly urbane Jewish accommodation. The website www.acommonword.org, a thoughtful Muslim equivalent.

Chief Rabbi Sachs has given us an excellent book, offering much balance and clear thinking in many respects. But he does unfortunately make religious pluralism a key part of his solution to the clash of civilizations. And in so doing, he tacitly banishes religious belief from the realm of knowledge to that of mere opinion.

But every serious religious teacher—from the Dali Lama to Eckhart Tolle, to take two contemporary examples—declares the nature of reality itself, not merely his or her opinions *about* reality.[1] Opinions are far too uncertain to sustain us in handling life's ultimate issues.

As Bishop Lesslie Newbigin said, faith cannot command our final and absolute allegiance—be our real religion—if we know it's "…only true for certain places and certain people. In a world which knows that there is only one physics and one mathematics, religion cannot do less than claim for its affirmations a like universal validity."[2]

And Dallas Willard concurs that belief only reliably governs life and action "…in its proper connection with knowledge and with the truth and evidence knowledge involves."[3] Mere opinion cannot possibly bear the weight of our lives.

The pluralist falsely assumes that admitting religion to the sphere of knowledge inevitably yields arrogance. But why is insisting that religious belief is only true for those who hold it any more gracious than seeing it as supported by a framework of sound understanding and knowledge? Atheists, pluralists, Buddhists and Hindus have amply demonstrated that monotheists have no monopoly on arrogance. Why does religion-as-knowledge require infallibility any more than, say, physics-as-knowledge?[4]

A friend named Carol once found herself carrying her hefty 14-month-old everywhere due to the fact that the little girl had broken her leg just days after taking her first steps. Such was her terror of walking that when her cast came off she utterly insisted on being carried. At first Carol gave in, but soon she saw that if she didn't steel herself to her daughter's sobs and tantrums, she'd be carrying her for years to come. Doing what *feels* kind isn't always kind. Sometimes it's a disaster for everyone involved.

This is true in all personal relationships. Extending help beyond healthy boundaries is unsustainable and hence counterproductive. It may look generous, but robbing Peter to pay Paul is never what it seems.

The very same thing is true of our truth boundaries. The pluralist's erasing of these boundaries to say all truth is one isn't actually loving. Only by keeping mercy and truth in tension do we truly retain either. The fundamentalist's sacrifice of love and mercy to "truth" and "justice" degenerates into glorified barbarism, neither true nor just. And the pluralist's sacrifice of truth to "love" leaves us bereft not just of truth, but ultimately of love too.

How can voting to relegate religion to the court of opinion possibly eliminate inter-religious conflict anyhow? What really are the odds of dogmatic pluralists wresting dogmatism from dogmatic Muslims like Osama bin Laden? The true middle ground is found in calling each other to discuss competing religious approaches— of which pluralism is one approach—honestly, humbly and graciously within the court of knowledge where they belong. Hardliners, whether fundamentalist or pluralist, may not listen. But for the sake of world peace, we must hope and pray they will.

Wanting just one human family, God began with one man and woman. This truth is found in both Bible and Qur'an. *Al-Hujurat* 13 says, "O mankind! We created you from a single pair—male and female—and made you into nations and tribes, that you might know each other, not that you might despise each other..." Regardless of race, religion or socio-economic class, we're all family.

God promised to bless all of earth's peoples through Abraham[5] and the psalmist says this is what God loves about Zion.[6] The preceding psalm says all nations will come and worship Yahveh.[7] And Isaiah speaks of the day when Egypt, Assyria and Israel will all be equally God's people.[8] Like Egypt and Assyria in Isaiah's day, Egypt and Babylon represented Israel's archenemies in the psalmist's day. And then as now, the Palestinians/Philistines its immediate threat. So this psalm is a radical celebration of the day when God brings all the nations together as one.[9]

Three times the psalmist says everyone will be "born in Zion."[10] Since everyone on earth can't literally be born in a single city, this has to refer to the spiritual rebirth we experience in knowing God. Not surprisingly, he says building a worldwide community where everyone has the very same access to God and knows him equally is ultimately a task he alone is up to.[11]

In his universal society, Yahveh is the source of everyone's life and blessing.[12] Again, this is because the whole earth comes to know him "…as the waters cover the sea," an event Isaiah links with the end of all violence and war.[13] Drawing their life from God makes them like him in character. No wonder they sing and dance for joy!

Prayer

Help me to believe you for the day when everyone knows you truly, from the least to the greatest, and in that knowledge the whole world finds its long lost oneness. And with it, all blessing and joy. Bring it soon, Lord! And help us not to give up hope however dark things look.   Amen.

90

On the Meaning of Life

[1]Lord, you've been our home
from time immemorial!
[2]Before earth gave birth to the mountains
from beginning to end you are God.

[3-5]A thousand years to you are like a day gone by.
An all-nighter lost to a moment's shut-eye.
You carry our years away as by flash flood
and then say, "Turn back, mortals!"
and back we go to dust.
We live and die like grass
[6]spring up fresh green in the morning
only to be scorched dry by nightfall.

[7]We're consumed by your anger—
your fury wears us out.
[8]You keep our rebellion on your radar
our secret sins* always in view.
[9]We live our lives in the heat of your glare
till they end with a sigh.
[10]We get 70 years, or 80 if our strength holds out.

But longer life only means more stress and strain
till our time is up and we're out of here.

[11]Who of us knows the full force of your anger
or lives with a fear to match it?
[12]Teach us to live like our days are numbered
and to seek your wisdom with heart and soul.

[13]Turn back, Yahveh!* How long?
Change your mind toward your servants!
[14]Flood us with your unfailing love at daybreak
so we can laugh and sing for the rest of our days.
[15]Give us good times
for as long as you've given us bad.
Joy equal to our pain.

[16]Let all of us who serve you
see you work powerfully in our lives
and our children see your glory revealed.
[17]May the smile of the Lord our God light up our lives.
And give lasting value to all that we do
so all that we do endures.

If, as the bumper sticker has it, "Life is hard and then you die,"
the question is *Is there any meaning to our troubled lives? Or is it
all just a crapshoot where we either enjoy the roll we're on or else
simply try to exit the game with dignity?*

In the affluent West, many use luxury and excitement to
escape life's misery. As these ebb, drugs and alcohol tend to flow.
Because apart from spirituality, we find what meaning we can in
material things.

With exotic powders, special kit, ritual practices, racy
vocabulary and risky rule breaking, the movie *Trainspotting* makes

an addict's existence very exciting. So it has been in the West since 19th century poet Samuel Coleridge "established the romantic connection between getting wasted on drugs and yet being granted the entree to a deeper reality than the rest of us get to see."[1] And what "loser" urging kids to *Just say NO* can possibly compete with that?

While hard drugs offer us wild escape, alcohol and pot can help us escape life too. But either way, we're missing the point which, as Clive James put it, is "that real life, with all its complications, is the only worthwhile mystery."[2] Yet we prolong this living death to avoid the honest reckoning that releases us to really live.

In contrast to Western materialism, Eastern traditions like Buddhism teach that as individuals, we're simultaneously meaningless blips on the screen of the Universe and the Universe itself, depending on which aspect of reality you're looking at. Either way, though, life's goal becomes mystically transcending our individuality. And we purchase our ticket for that through supreme discipline in both moral virtues and spiritual techniques.

All is One, so *good = evil = creation = nothing*. Since suffering is such a big part of life, it's left us to simply seek a "meaningful" exit from it. However many lives it takes us to attain that.

But combine the wisdom of a Buddhist master like Thich Nhat Hanh with the usefulness of many Buddhist meditative practices. Throw in the personal charisma of the Dalai Lama. And suddenly contradictions like *everything = nothing* start sounding plausible. Especially to people fed up with the biblical answers so typically disdained by our media.

So we convince ourselves as John Lennon did that the East is the way out. We may even follow him in adding Eastern religion to our drugs and drink. But where does *exit = no exit* like in the East?

The psalmist's view is radically different. He admits life is hard and death comes far too swiftly. And he battles the sense of futility that suggests. But he sees God's anger as key here. If the everlasting God is the context of both human life and death,[3] it makes perfect sense that we live our lives under either his glare or his smile.

For the psalmist to make God's anger the cause of suffering and death will strike many as stupid. Like he's only digging himself in deeper. But the real problem is sin. Living in a fallen world exacts its toll, whether through catastrophe, accident, illness or death.

Some suffering—though by no means all—comes as the effect of specific sins, whether by the simple outworking of physical or spiritual laws or by acts of divine judgment. Driving your car off a cliff, for example, is usually deadly. As well, sins like worry, greed, bitterness, betrayal and workaholism have profound psychosomatic effects, causing such things as stomach ulcers, headaches and depression. However normal or natural our sins "feel," we weren't designed for them. We may not know that but our bodies unerringly do.

Suffering is by no means always the result of our sins, though. Disease often strikes randomly. Though clearly innocent, some babies are born with debilitating congenital defects. And most accidents and natural disasters strike without divine intervention. All because, provoking God's righteous anger as it did, our first parents' sin plunged our entire world into suffering and death.

Just hearing this infuriates many people. But denying God's existence or making him a bit player in our own personal New Age production doesn't take away his anger or the pain resulting from it. Taking God's anger seriously is far more productive.

That's what the psalmist does.[4] Knowing God is merciful and compassionate, he urges him to do an about-face and show mercy instead of judgment. In effect he says, "Enough, Lord! Switch your program from pain to joy. And not just momentarily either!" He wants one full day of joy for every day of pain they've endured.

God's unfailing love for his people is what makes him so bold as to ask for this. But he knows there has to be change on our side too—an honest acceptance that our days really are numbered.[5] Heidegger said living well means living as if each day was our last.[6] Living like that makes us seek wisdom with all our heart. And living by God's wisdom enriches our lives as he invests all we do with lasting value.

We all long for God's wisdom and truth. But even we who openly declare God's way to be best find ourselves deep down believing we know better. All we can do when that lie rears its head is renounce it anew and ask for cleansing and grace.

Embracing God doesn't mean we get answers to all the questions we can think of. But dissolving all our questions in a mix of materialism, drugs and mystical nothingness is hardly helpful. Better far the freedom and joy we find in opening our hearts to God's unfathomable wisdom. Only he can keep us honest to our own self-destructiveness and the lies we so sincerely embrace. Living life in honest dependence on him, we're at home in the God who, transcending time and space, is the source of all meaning.

Prayer

Your understanding far surpasses mine, Lord. Yet though you are Wisdom itself, I so often trust my judgment over yours and blind myself to what I do. Forgive me. Teach me how short my time here is and how desperately I need you. Light up my life, I pray. Amen.

91

The Poetry of Faith

[1]Whoever lives in the secret place of God Most High
rests secure in the shadow of the Almighty.
[2]I will say this of Yahveh:*
he's my refuge and fortress
the kind of God you can really trust.

[3]He will surely rescue you
from deadly ambush and epidemic.
[4]He'll shelter you in his warm embrace
safe beneath his outspread wings.
His faithfulness will be your shield and armor.
[5]You will not fear the terrors of the night
nor sniper fire in broad daylight.
[6]You will not fear the plague that stalks in darkness
nor sudden death at midday.
[7]Though 1,000 fall on your left
and 10,000 on your right
when it's all over
you're still standing—unscathed
[8]a solemn witness to how evildoers get repaid in full.
[9]Since you've made Yahveh your refuge

the Most High your home
[10]no disaster will strike you
nor will tragedy track you down.
[11]Because he's ordered his angels
to guard you wherever you go.
[12]They'll lift you up in their hands
lest you stub your toe on a rock.
[13]You'll trample on lions and snakes unharmed—
even lions in their prime and deadly serpents.

[14]"Because they love me," says Yahveh
"I'll rescue them.
I'll set them in safety because they cling to me.
[15]When they call on me
I'll answer them.
I'll be with them when trouble strikes
to rescue and honor them.
[16]With long life will I satisfy them
and grant them my salvation."

The young David went from national hero to outlaw overnight. He spent the years that followed running up and down desolate canyons west of the Dead Sea with the rabidly jealous Saul and his army in hot pursuit.

All of this psalm's images could be talking about David during his fugitive years. With Saul on one side of the mountain and David on the other, nothing Saul did to catch him ever worked. Even when Saul and his bodyguard entered the cave David was hiding in, it was Saul—not David—whose life was at risk.[1]

Back then epidemics often produced more field army casualties than armed combat did. But though perpetually on the move, David's band of soldiers grew stronger every year. Camping in the wild, the haunt of both lions and serpents, God protected them from both.[2]

In what could have been David's worst blunder ever, he ran away from running away by joining the Philistine army, Israel's nemesis. In the ensuing battle Saul was killed along with Jonathan, his son and David's soul mate. Had David fought in that battle, it would have haunted him for life. But doubting his loyalty, the Philistine generals sent him home instead, leaving him a solemn witness to the slaughter on both sides.[3]

Best of all, the more Saul did to dishonor David the more God increased David's stature in the eyes of his people.[4] Till David won their hearts and they crowned him king.

That kind of context helps me get past my offense over how categorical the psalm's promises sound. Whether or not David was its writer is moot. Regardless, it was written by someone who had seen God care for him in every possible way and who can't help but commend his faithfulness to others.

I'm afraid we in the 21st century aren't terribly encouraged by this, however. We see the psalm's promises of safety day and night and ask how the 16-year-old is to read it the day she comes home from being date raped. How her parents should read it when they learn what happened.

What help is God's promise when they march you off to the gas chamber in Auschwitz? What if he promises honor and care but allows your enemies to build yet more settlements on what little is left of your ancestral lands? Where are his protecting angels when your husband beats you, trashes your home and calls you every vile name he knows? How can God say he'll spare us the plague and allow babies to be born HIV-positive?

"But it's not promised to everyone," someone cautions. "Only to those who love Yahweh. Being born into a faith community isn't enough. It all hinges on whether or not you live in Yahweh's presence."[5]

Then how well must we love God for it to work? If the answer is "perfectly" and nobody can, what good is that? What good are promises that fail you in your time of need? When you're hanging over a precipice and God holds out a broken branch—something that works only some of the time—is that the best he can do?

There are three different ways to read this psalm. First, literally. That our lives will be immune to all trouble if we serve God. But that doesn't square with many biblical stories—of Joseph, Job, David or Jeremiah, who trusted God in the midst of unjust sufferings. If perfect protection requires perfect trust, then the psalm speaks only of God's *intention* toward us. And while that's great to know, it ends up sounding like gross overstatement since we live in a real, not ideal, world.

Second, we can read it as hyperbole, overstatement for effect. There's undeniably lots of figurative language here. God doesn't have a physical body, so he can't have a literal—physical—shadow or wings. The numbers 1,000 and 10,000 are figurative. Things like "trampling" on lions and serpents may be figurative. But if there's an element of overstatement throughout, then what does it really amount to? What can we hold God to contractually?

Third, we can read it eschatologically, as if it speaks literally, but only of the final deliverance when God puts everything right in the world and welcomes us to our eternal home. If it all refers to the future, though, what good is it now?

As you may already have guessed, we must answer the question *do we read the psalm literally, figuratively or eschatologically?* with a resounding *yes*. All of these approaches are complementary, according to Mark Futato, each providing a window on the truth.[6] This is poetry, after all—not a legal code.

There is hyperbole, but it's meant to increase our faith in Yahveh right here in this imperfect world. And even there literal fulfillment is possible. For example, the prophet Daniel literally stepped on ravenous lions and came out unharmed.[7] Beyond that, the psalm invites us to believe God will ultimately make everything right.

We can't expect him to protect us from every foolish choice we make. Nor does trusting him guarantee we'll never suffer unjustly. But the psalm's imagery inspires us to trust him in a way no legal contract ever could. To trust both that his intentions toward us are wholly good and that he's in control and will yet deliver us. Even if deliverance looks way different and takes way longer than we think it should.

In an age of human rights, we want law, not poetry. But poetry soars high above law. And like all poets, the psalmist speaks to the heart, leaving the head to catch up as it can.[8] So we must choose. We can join the cynics who snort and rail. Or we can let God be God, marvel that he bothers with us at all and ask him to help us trust him, whatever doubts we have.

Prayer

Help me live in the shelter of your presence, Lord. Along with David, Esther, Daniel, Sojourner Truth, Aleksandr Solzhenitsyn and a vast host of others, I believe you grant me a freedom and dignity no one can strip me of. That you watch over me, can somehow turn evil into good and will one day make everything right. Lord, I believe—help me overcome my unbelief!   Amen.

100

Song of Joy

[1]Shout for joy to Yahveh,* all the earth!
[2]Worship Yahveh with gladness.
Come with joyful songs.

[3]Honor Yahveh as God.
He is our Maker—we are his people
the flock that he shepherds.

[4]Enter his gates with thanksgiving
and fill his courts with praise.
Give thanks to him and praise his name
[5]because Yahveh is good.
His love endures forever—
his faithfulness through all generations.

The word *religion* evokes strong reactions from many people today. Some involuntarily grit their teeth since the only religion they know is endless slogging to save their soul—typically with the threat of hellfire hanging over them if they ever slack off.

Others inwardly grimace at its mention since to them it's just the complete opposite of fun, composed of long lists of do's and don'ts, replete with angry frowns and generous doses of guilt, shame and pretense. How, they ask, could heaven be fun if religion is any sort of prelude?

Religion's mention makes still others want to hurl their lunch. They've read too many articles like last week's in the *Vancouver Sun* about a local evangelical church that hid rather than exposed a known sexual predator—or today's on the BBC website, virtually identical except that all the players are Muslims in Abu Dhabi. Maybe they've even lived the horror themselves in some way or other.

To all these people, this psalm seems only to add to the pretence. Because if religion and joy have nothing in common, then the psalmist is inviting us to sing about joy with no chance of experiencing it. And that's got to be fun!

A lot of organized religion, though, is so wide of the mark that its connection to true religion is only superficial. It has all its outer trappings—which are all too easily institutionalized —but without its power, life or joy. No wonder so many want nothing to do with it. But are these reductions really all religion amounts to? Or is it not that by limiting religion to its worst expressions we can more easily dispose of it?

As much as I sympathize with many despisers of religion, I'm convinced they throw the baby out with the bathwater. Like sex, religion can do as much harm as good. Some people use sex to buy love, others to numb the pain where they've been emotionally wounded. Others to lash out in violence. Still others are addicted to sex and live for the nanosecond when their death-dealing craving stops.

But the fact that abusive sex wounds and deadens rarely keeps us from seeking the other kind of sex, the healing and fulfilling kind that borders on heaven itself. Aside from the mentally ill, we don't swear off *all* sex simply because *bad* sex abounds. It only teaches us to think carefully about the sort of sex we seek.

Likewise true religion's power to heal and fulfill is often perverted. But should this surprise us? Anything as powerful as either sex or religion is bound to have its abusers. It simply urges caution lest we settle for a distorted version that resembles the true, but has lost all its goodness and joy.

Many say here, "Thanks, but no thanks. I am spiritual, but I'm just not into organized religion." What they're really saying is: When it comes to spirituality I'll do things my way. And in the hyper-individualism of the West, this has huge appeal. We're bent on doing things our way and distrust the big story, the big picture, the big everything.

But these narrowed horizons shut out the larger spiritual context of our story, making my story and yours really small-time. They also rob us of any larger context for the tangible oneness of community with its healing touch. Because no one is in the same story we're in, no one outside ourselves can effectively challenge or correct us. But none of us were meant to be Lone Rangers.

Saying we're for world peace, but not for spiritual community is like saying we love sailing but will have nothing to do with boats. Without that basic commitment, we can't share the rhythm of the journey, nor the responsibilities and joys of a life that's larger than just ours. And this greatly reduces all our spiritual celebrations, making them like solo parties.

It is possible to fashion for yourself something roughly equivalent to organized religion out of your own imagination, with a few like-minded friends. But it's work-intensive and either falls far short of spiritual effectiveness or else runs into the very same commitment issues that keep us from joining religious groups.

So many who have been burnt by organized religion can't bear to think of going back. Others are so disturbed by the state it's in that they want nothing to do with it. God undoubtedly understands all such avoidance. But his answer is healing, justice and communal change, not measured rebellion.

The real question here is *what does God want us to do?* There's no question that he's concerned about his people, his own flock. That's clear in scripture from Genesis on. But what if he wants us to make a difference? What if, to borrow Gandhi's words, God wants *us* to be the change we wish to see in our church, synagogue or mosque?

As the psalmist makes clear, worship is just as much corporate as private and personal. On one hand, it's meant to be part of the warp and woof of our everyday lives, practiced informally in small groups and in solitude too. But on the other hand, it reaches its fullest expression only in the large group.

Where hostile governments forbid its larger expressions, worship can go underground and limit itself to whatever size or shape is necessary. But this psalm is not the only one that calls worshippers to come together *en masse* to fill Yahveh's courts with praise.

In a culture as individualistic as ours, corporate worship has built-in problems. For one thing, it's hard for some of us to imagine anything involving the whole group as truly authentic. But the key thing here is that we approach *God* in worship. Whether my mind wanders momentarily or I fully appreciate the words I sing isn't the issue. Even limping, you can run a marathon, so long as you stay the course.

It's been many centuries since the temple in Jerusalem was destroyed. But the fact remains that giving our corporate worship a visible place in the public sphere is important, our society's growing distaste for it notwithstanding. For us to limit our expressions of worship for the sake of comfort or convenience really does miss the point. Worship is always about God's pleasure first and foremost and ours only second.

It's in encountering him that we truly discover joy. Psalm 16:11 says, "…you fill me with joy in your presence…" To be welcomed into God's presence, surrounded by his people—all with no pretense whatsoever—is heaven itself, the very pinnacle of joy. This is what Yahveh invites us to. He has no interest in joyless religion replete with bottled smiles and phony love.

He's made us his own. So we praise him for being so determinedly on our side. We thank him for his unfailing goodness and love. We let loose and sing for joy.

Prayer

Free me, Lord, from that contempt for your people that masquerades as spirituality but really is born of pride. You're the One who made us your people. So let me join them in worshipping you with all my heart. Let me bow in adoration, weep tears of gratitude and sing for joy. Fill me with your contagious joy, I pray. Amen.

103

Awesome God

¹Praise Yahveh, * *heart and soul!*
Praise his holy name!
²Praise Yahveh, heart and soul
and forget none of his good gifts!

³He forgives all your sins*
and heals all your diseases.
⁴He rescues you from disaster
and crowns you with undying mercy and love.
⁵He satisfies you with good things
and renews your strength like an eagle's.
⁶Yahveh works relentlessly
to vindicate and release all the oppressed.
⁷He revealed his ways to Moses
his actions to the Israelites.
⁸Yahveh is merciful and gracious
slow to get angry and overflowing in faithful love.
⁹He doesn't hold grudges or endlessly accuse.
¹⁰In fact, he doesn't repay us in kind
or treat us as our sins deserve.
¹¹As vast as the heavens' farthest reach

so vast is his unrelenting love for all who fear him.
[12]As far as east is from west
so far has he removed our sins from us.
[13]Like a good father is gentle with his children
so Yahveh has compassion on all who fear him
[14]knowing full well what we're made of—dust.
[15]Mere mortals, we're like field flowers
 that blaze into life
[16]only to be blown away by the wind
leaving no trace behind.
[17]But Yahveh's relentless love
for those who fear him
knows neither beginning nor end.
And his salvation
belongs to the children and grandchildren
[18]of all who keep his covenant
and obey its commandments.

[19]With his throne founded
in the heavens high above
Yahveh's kingdom rules over all!

[20]Praise Yahveh
all you mighty angels who obey his every command!
[21]Praise Yahveh
all you heavenly armies who please him in every way!
[22]Praise Yahveh
all he's created everywhere throughout all his domains!
And me too: *Praise Yahveh, heart and soul!*

For years now people have been saying God is dead—and with a myriad of different meanings. But however sick and infirm he may be, this God lives on in our culture. Mainly because stereotypes die so hard.

One stereotype better laid to rest is the God of angry, vindictive justice. This was the one the great reformer Martin Luther lived in mortal fear of before encountering God's grace. This deity can't make your life miserable enough, blows you out of the water without even trying and can't wait for you to mess up for him to do so.

At the other end of the spectrum is the watered-down, I'm-OK-you're-OK milquetoast God who never objects, no matter how we live. If only he had the power to match his love! Present wherever we are, he makes things go our way whenever he can, but he mostly just wrings his hands in the background. So don't count on him for help.

Flat as they are, these Gods are just too small. They don't make sense either. Because how could Yahveh be just, require us to love each other and yet be vindictive himself? On the other hand, how could he be truly loving and turn a blind eye to the axe murderer's crime? Non-confrontational, spineless, wishy-washy and confused—yes. But hardly loving when it comes to the victim.

Then there are those who fuse these stereotypes together to come up with a third God, who plays vicious monster one minute and feeble lover the next, but is mostly just moody and unpredictable. This God is everyone's worst nightmare. So anyone assuring us he's a bad dream we've now awakened from is doing us a kindness. And how could such a Jekyll-and-Hyde keep the universe on track for even a single day?

Against all such stereotypical Gods, the psalmist speaks of a God who is very much alive, one whose endless love and justice are mysteriously one. Though he knows how weak we are, he's not at all out to get us. Instead he's compassionate like a loving father with his little child. And fast fading as our glory is, he still longs for our love.

That said, he won't tolerate our sin. As the psalmist puts it, it angers him. But still he doesn't endlessly finger us or harbor grudges. He wants not to damn us, but to release us from the sin and guilt that so mercilessly oppress us. Even when we fail him, he's slow to get angry. Rather, he lavishes on us the very opposite of what our sins deserve—sheer mercy.[1]

This will sound like injustice to some. Because if God accepts us unconditionally, how can he not accept axe murderers too? The truth is: he does, but only if they truly throw themselves on his mercy. Then he's more than willing to remove their sins from them, as far as east from west. But to truly throw ourselves on his mercy means submitting to him as Lord. Because if he rescued us not *from* our sins, but somehow *with all our sins in tow,* what kind of rescue would that be?

How can he do this and still be just? The psalmist doesn't say. But he mentions three things that point to an answer. First, he speaks of God's revelation of himself to Israel under Moses.[2] Within the context of covenant, he showed his people something of how the tension between his mercy and his justice plays out. That included rescuing them from slavery, being present with them—to guide, provide for, protect, discipline and heal them— and giving them his law with its sacrificial offerings.[3]

That was his way of putting redemption right at the heart of his plan for creation—not as some sort of add-on. Frankly, this God may be messier than we want and we may never fully comprehend how he can be just and yet pardon the guilty. But any lesser God would not deserve our worship.

The psalmist also speaks of the community of faith.[4] Because salvation always comes to us in the shape of a community. But having seen how brutal organized religion can be, we hesitate to commit to church, synagogue or mosque. Our culture's hyper-individualism makes me wonder why God can't just accept me as a "group of one." Or makes me ask that God save me and my friends apart from some clunky, multi-generational religious club.

But the community of faith was never to be a club of smug, self-satisfied people. And salvation isn't just a gift I receive. It's a life I'm called to live simultaneously in three dimensions: in God's presence, in the community of God-seekers and in the world at large. And to whatever degree I turn away from any of those dimensions, I've gone back to making myself the center of the universe.

Last, the psalmist points to God's sovereign rule over all.[5] This means not only that he's in charge but that all mysteries are ultimately explained in him.

The richness of God's grace to him leaves the psalmist awestruck. So he ends with the very same line of self-talk he began with. It first sounded like someone starting a cold engine, but it ends up a happy cry of praise to the God who rules over all and yet humbly stoops to rescue the weak and broken. And that's because the psalmist consciously joins the vast multitudes of angels and everything else in creation that knows how truly great our God is.

Prayer

Who am I, Lord, that the King of creation should love me and tirelessly seek my love? Yet rebel that I am, you've forgiven my sins and are releasing me from oppression, making me whole. So with heart and soul, I join with your people and with all creation in worshipping you, our awesome God. Amen.

110

God on Our Side

¹Yahveh's* word to my lord was this:
    "Sit enthroned beside me
      while I make your enemies your footstool."
²It is Yahveh
who extends the scepter of your authority from Zion.*
Rule triumphant, though encircled by foes!
³Your people will rally behind you
when kissed by the dew of your youth
you lead your troops out on the holy mountains
at dawn's first blush.

⁴Yahveh has sworn irrevocably:
"You are a priest forever in Melchizedek's royal order."
⁵The Lord stands right by your side
crushing rebel kings on the day of his anger.
⁶He executes judgment on the nations
stacks valleys high with corpses
cracks skulls the whole world over.
⁷And pausing to drink from a brook by the way
he moves on in triumph.

No biblical truth is either more heartening or more problematic than the concept of God being "on our side." Heartening because it means we're not left to our own devices. And God's help goes beyond merely saving us as isolated individuals—as if that was possible—to include his accomplishing his redemptive purposes for our world.

When I think of people like British MP William Wilberforce, Gandhi, Catholic social activist Dorothy Day, Martin Luther King Jr., Mother Theresa and Nobel prize-winning Bangladeshi banker Muhammad Yunus, I'm so glad God blesses those who do his work. Whether we stand in the limelight or play our part in obscurity, if we bring great love to any good work, it is God who does his work through us.

But as comforting as that is, this truth is open to gross abuse, leading to one of the ugliest aspects of monotheism as it exists in our world. The idea that we of all people somehow have God on a tow rope, such that he automatically blesses us no matter what we do.

What makes this so ugly is its utter arrogance, one that never remotely questions why God might not endorse all our opinions and choices. Whether we invade Iraq[1] or another non-threatening country, enact laws to force the homeless off our streets, consign the Gaza Strip's 1.6 million residents to a prison camp existence or spend profligately on ourselves with no thought of the environment, "it's all good!" This can only mean we've turned God into an American, Canadian, Israeli or whatever else. But who has time for such paltry implications when we're so busy planning our next move, purchase or pursuit, assured that God will bless it whatever it is?

So absurdly egomaniacal is this concept of divine blessing it would be laughable if it wasn't so sad. But it's not even remotely biblical. That we're sold on some aspect of our own culture hardly means God sees things as we do. If sin taints all our thoughts—and it does, biblically speaking—that would make God's thinking as tainted as ours is. In fact, he'd need salvation too!

While this sort of arrogance often accompanies civil religion, we mustn't equate seeking God's blessing on our country with taking his endorsement for granted. It's always right for a nation to seek God's blessing—as does "God Bless America" and the British and Canadian national anthems. But when we go on from there to assume that God *unreservedly* approves of our government or institutions, we make an impossible leap. God is perfect, after all. Nothing we do ever is.

That's not to suggest he only blesses perfection. Not at all. He continually blesses our weak and imperfect efforts to please him. But however much he permits evil to prosper, he never blesses or condones it. And the reality is that we, his people, are all too often involved in evil.

However insistently we say a war is right doesn't make it right. However legally we rob the poor or hoard our wealth, never makes it ethical. This proneness to miss God's path even while we're convinced we're on it is what makes it imperative that we keep scripture in mind both day and night.[2] It alone gives us clear understanding of God's thinking on all we say and do—what he will and won't bless. Even then, we so easily make God's Word say what we want it to. We need rather to approach it humbly and be genuinely open to the correction of others too.

How can God bless all we do when scripture so clearly teaches that he has no favorites? He invites everyone everywhere to know and enjoy his blessing on the same basic terms. Even in the psalmist's day, anyone who submitted to Yahveh was blessed by him. Israel clearly had unique status as God's covenant people. But that never excluded non-Israelites from knowing Yahveh.

If God somehow blessed Americans, Canadians or Israelis on other terms than he had for everyone else, that would be favoritism. But his terms for all of us alike are justice, mercy and humility always—all of which are the outworking of his free grace to us.

The psalmist here pictures a coronation where Yahveh blesses his appointed king, who he refers to as "my lord."[3] That Yahveh tells him he'll wage war at his side isn't unusual. A king's being military commander-in-chief was standard back then.[4]

It's remarkable that Yahveh designates him a priest also because these two offices were distinct in ancient Israel.[5] Kings were never to offer sacrifices or usurp other priestly duties. Neither were priests to rule.

In another sense, though, it's not all that remarkable because under Moses the entire nation was called to be "a royal priesthood." That is, all God's people were to exercise his rule on his behalf *and* to bless and offer the world to him in worship. God's inauguration of a class of priests and later on of kings to lead the nation in serving him was never meant to alter that.

This idea of royal priesthood points back to the Melchizedek the psalmist mentions. He was both Jerusalem's king and God's priest back in Abraham's day.[6] But we needn't take the idea of Melchizedek's "order" literally, as if he founded an actual priestly order. Along with his royal authority, God simply meant to endow the king with Melchizedek's priestly role of blessing and offering the creation back to God. Melchizedek generously blessed Abraham for doing the right thing. That is, for putting the welfare of the oppressed above his own welfare. Abraham trusted God to help him overthrow evil and release the captives. That was what Melchizedek blessed.

Verse 4 is the psalm's focal point and must interpret the whole for us. What precedes it is the assurance of victory no matter how hopeless it looks. Because God is on this king's side as he battles against evil and releases captives.[7] God is the one who rallies his troops around him and, through him, defeats his enemies. It's almost as if verse 4 fuses together Abraham with Melchizedek. The one leads a vastly outnumbered army that proves irresistible, while the other serves as God's royal priest blessing Abraham's weary foot soldiers both physically and spiritually.

What follows verse 4 is a grisly picture of the universal scope of Yahveh's judgment. As in Psalm 2, all the rebellious nations are made to submit as Yahveh and his anointed king stack valleys high with corpses, cracking skulls all over the world and doing so easily, handily.[8]

The psalm nowhere states who Yahveh's designated priest-king is. But this is clearly the great day of Yahveh's anger. And the king is Yahveh's vicegerent under him, his ally in the decisive military campaign to crush all earthly rebellion once and for all. As verse 7 implies, Yahveh will not end his clean-up operation till it's totally finished.[9] So this isn't just any king. It's Yahveh's promised Messiah.

But what's true of him is true of us also. As long as we fight the same fight that Abraham fought, we too can count on God's being on our side. We may not always appear to have the upper hand, but we actually do, provided we faithfully follow his lead in the fight.

As Jim Wallis puts it, the real issue is whether or not we're on God's side.[10] Bearing the same joint royal-priestly role as the Messiah, we bless our fellow foot soldiers and advance as Yahveh uses us to execute his judgment and release captives.

Prayer

Forgive our arrogant strutting, God, as if we—not you—were in control. Give us hearts wide open to you, moved by the things that move your heart. Help us believe you won't stop till our world is home to both justice and peace. Yes, help us to live in hope, Lord. Hope that looks for the dawn when the sky is still black. Amen.

120

In the Desperate Pause Between Wars[1]

[1]I called to Yahveh* in desperation
and he answered me.
[2]Deliver me, Yahveh
from lips that lie
and tongues that twist.

[3]Can't you see what you'll get
from your deception?
[4]Fiery ruin—
a hailstorm of missiles
that's what!

[5]How wretched to be stuck in Pyongyang
Mogadishan warlords on every hand!
[6]Far too long have I lived
among people who hate peace.
[7]I long for peace
but whenever I speak out
they are for war.

When Gainesville, Florida, Pastor Terry Jones threatened to host a public—even *ritual*—burning of the Qur'an, we might have expected it to make local news. But who would have thought he'd hold the whole world spellbound for days? In our post-9-11 radioactivity, though, it became world news and then very nearly a tragedy in the making as Muslims all over the globe responded vehemently. Thank God Iran doesn't yet have nuclear capability.

At the same time it was a comedy of errors, Jones being the kid who, wanting a bit of attention, lit a firecracker only to find the fuse connected to a ton of TNT. This had to have startled him more than anyone else. Staging a local publicity stunt to vent his wrath and boost church attendance, he finds the whole world breathing down his neck. Because unbeknownst to him, his threat is an act of war.

Jones's behavior deeply saddened, but didn't shock me. Nor does the fact that he wrote a book attacking "Islam" in vitriolic terms. Many others have done the same. Neither am I shocked that hundreds of people sent him copies of the Qur'an for burning. Sad to say, there's a little Qur'an-burning in a lot of people. Muslim-Christian history has been a love-hate relationship from the first. And there have been recent documented cases of Muslims elsewhere doing to Bibles precisely what Jones threatened to do to the Qur'an.

What makes a person in the 21st century burn someone else's holy book? The answer, I believe, is a desperate mix of ignorance, prejudice, anger and fear. Combine that with our own opportunistic ambitions and you have something far more lethal than we know.

Fear and anger so easily blind us to critical details and rob us of whatever emotional intelligence we have. They also rob us of the grace to humbly acknowledge good things about others and their scriptures, lest we're somehow mistaken as "endorsing" them. So we see only evil.

Another part of the problem lies in the way we turn the

world's 1.5 billion Muslims into an imaginary entity called "Islam." This then serves as a fixed target and enables us to paint all Muslims with one brush.

But the fact is, "Islam" doesn't really exist—not like that. Each Muslim in the world has his or her own understanding of the Qur'an, of God and, yes, of Islam. Everyone believes somewhat differently from everyone else. Even within individuals, understandings and beliefs fluctuate. So to treat all our Muslim brothers and sisters as a monolith is unhelpful and plays into the hands of our foes.

Lest this idea seem foreign, let me candidly admit that the very same is true of Christianity. We blithely cover a vast range of diversity with the name "Christianity." But as useful as such shorthand is in some contexts, Christianity is an imaginary construct that blurs all our many distinctions into one.[2] And the same can be said of "Judaism" and all the other faiths.

We all use such terms at times and I'm not saying we shouldn't. But I would certainly argue that whenever we do use them, we should do so intelligently, thoughtfully, carefully. They can be loaded terms—can so easily do more harm than good.

Ignorance of people just like ourselves tells us "Islam" is the force making Muslims do what they do. Granted, beliefs and group dynamics play a huge role in religion, not least with the Muslim faith. One person's faith or fear can influence others profoundly. But again, reifying the faith of so many millions of people often distorts more than clarifies.[3]

Thankfully, both Presidents George W. Bush and Barack Obama have insisted that America is *not* at war with Islam, but only with radical Muslim elements like al-Qaida and the Taliban. How much wiser is that than the position of former U.S. Speaker of the House, Newt Gingrich. Decrying what he calls "stealth jihad"—a supposedly covert Muslim socio-political offensive designed to undermine and destroy American civilization—Gingrich takes a McCarthyesque approach, where mere association establishes guilt.[4] That's the last thing we need in an atmosphere so emotionally charged.

Fear is a huge problem for us all—Muslim and non-Muslim alike. Witness the way the announcement by a group of moderate Muslims to build a cultural center and mosque near Ground Zero[5] has fueled our society's latent fear of Islam. Labeling the project's name "triumphalist," Gingrich condemned it as part of the über-threat of America's Islamicization[6]

But the moderates behind the center insist that Osama bin Laden has hijacked the Islamic agenda and stolen their Muslim identity on them. To them there's nothing at all triumphalist about the name "Cordoba House." Instead Cordoba represents the high point in Islamic history in terms of both cultural achievement and tolerance of others. And that at a time when European Christians regularly burned heretics at the stake. With today's headlines up for grabs, though, what ambitious pastor or politician has time for such minutia? Clearly ignorance, opportunism and fear can make us "...falsely accuse people who live peaceably in the land."[7]

Regrettably one judge's ruling left New Jersey's Muslim women unprotected against marital rape for a short while. The judge ruled that a Muslim husband's repeated sexual assaults against his wife were legal since the man's imam had testified that Shariah law permits them. Thankfully, that ruling was quickly overturned by a superior court,[8] demonstrating that any threat of America's being Islamicized is a long way off. But millions of Americans still genuinely fear it.[9]

Another vital question is how we're going to approach the Muslim faith. Gingrich complains that most secular American universities give a patently propagandistic presentation and I believe he's right in terms of most undergraduate programs.[10] This is because reification invariably chooses one stream or form— the one that best suits our particular socio-political or theological purposes—and makes it the whole. The majority of our educators present a peace-loving Islam that fits with their pluralism and downplays serious differences between Muslims and the rest of us.[11] Our pro-Zionists present an equally one-sided version of Islam, though, the militant one that conservative Catholic Gingrich and charismatic Jones attack.[12] The fact is, both versions are true.

Unfortunately, dealing only in half-truths, both approaches muddy the waters of national debate and create a climate of mutual distrust. This naturally increases the polarization now threatening not just our society, but our entire world order. One wonders how anyone can think such distortion will lead to the win-win solution we so desperately need.[13]

With American troops fighting Muslim extremists overseas, with Iran as America's bitterest foe and with the recurring televisation of fiery al-Qaida threats to take over America, 9-11 lives on in our wounded collective psyche. Akhbar Ahmed rightly observes that we've reached the place in America where everyone feels they're a victim.[14] Whites, Muslims, African-Americans, Hispanics—everyone. This does not bode well for us, especially given the emotional ignorance some of our leaders display.

With similar challenges facing every Western society, how can we move forward? Only by real truth telling—a very unpopular pastime apparently—and by holding fast to three things that have indisputably made America great. The first is its openness to outsiders, New York City being the prime example here. The second is its strong commitment to human rights, premiere among them being religious freedom for all—which must include freedom for all law-abiding Muslim citizens. And the third is a lifelong vigilance against anything in others *or in ourselves* which threatens either of the first two distinctives.[15]

To give any of these things up would not only *please* al-Qaida, it would *mimic* al-Qaida. Surely the path of grace, truth and mutual understanding is the only way forward, no matter how hard it is. This is where heartfelt prayer is so vital. Prayer like the psalmist's above.

Prayer

As politicians, pastors, generals, industrialists and ordinary citizens, we can so easily misrepresent and falsely accuse others for opportunistic reasons. Misrepresent ourselves too. Forgive us, Lord, for making peace just the pause between our wars. Give us hearts that refuse the fear threatening to undo us, mouths that speak the truth in love and feet that unflinchingly walk the path of peace, however hard it be. Amen.

126

The Law of Attraction

¹When Yahveh* restored Zion's* fortunes
we felt sure we were dreaming.
²Our lives became torrents of laughter and song.
Even pagan neighbors exclaimed
"Yahveh's done awesome things for them!"
³But it was no dream —
he did such awesome things our joy overflowed.

⁴Turn our lives around again, Yahveh
like dry rivers turned to floods.

⁵Those who plant with tears will reap with joy.
⁶Yes, those who plant their seed weeping
will dance the harvest home to songs of joy!

With everyone running after Madison Avenue's pimped dreams
of glamour and affluence, who can keep up? Often those who
can't—and even those who can—find themselves in a place of
desolation like the one this psalm is written from, where they don't
know if they can take another step and they're desperate for relief.
Because while the rat race offers bits and pieces—health, wealth,

pleasure, intellectual stimulation, sexual fulfillment, etc.—it has nothing at the core to hold everything together.

This is where we're tempted to view spirituality very pragmatically as a way to get some wholeness along with all the stuff we want. Wicca and other nature-based religions fall into this category, but two more popular approaches here represent alternative versions of "prosperity consciousness," with roots in 19th-century Christian Science.

Many New Age gurus proclaim the "law of attraction," which holds that like attracts like and makes the universe around us just the physical manifestation of our thoughts. So to gain health, wealth and success, we must simply think what we want.

In *The Secret*, for example, master marketer Rhonda Byrne renders her think-and-grow-rich scheme down to a handy three-step formula of asking, believing and receiving. But you must also assiduously replace all negative thoughts with gratitude for what you have and visualization of what you want. Do this and you get your desires—no *ifs, ands* or *buts.*

Capital-y "You" design your own destiny, says Byrne. You have the final say on the kind of life You will live. Because everything that is—earth, sun, moon, stars—all exists for You. In fact, without You it couldn't exist. Add to this, organized religion's self-serving conspiracy to "cover up" this "age-old" wisdom and, bingo, the universe delivers wealth and fame. At least to Byrne, who ends her best-selling book assuring readers that this knowledge—that the universe, the kingdom, all of life belongs to us—is the secret everyone longs to know.[1]

Though in many respects the polar opposite of this New Age gospel, the other popular version of prosperity consciousness comes in the gospel many televangelists preach. Having long championed God's power to heal and bless, our Pentecostal and charismatic brothers and sisters are generally more open than other Christians to Christian Science's redefinition of faith.

Convince them that they exercise this "faith" for the honor of God's name and an apparently noble passion overtakes them, obscuring its underlying addictions.

Affirming historic creeds, these preachers wouldn't dream of making capital-y You the center of the universe as Byrne does. But they may just be less honest there. Because the selfishness of their gospel is clear to almost everyone else.

Truthfulness isn't always the point here though. Where, for example, does refusing to accept the finality of your doctor's diagnosis end and the denial of your actual physical condition begin? Because along with gratitude, praise and visualization, the prosperity gospel emphasizes both talking and acting like that future miracle is already yours. This makes talking about negative symptoms a threat to faith—that is, till you're healed and they're suddenly marshaled as proofs of God's healing power. While there is some truth here, there's also a major redefinition of faith, holiness and more.

Making self so central crowds out loving relationships and can lead to "exuberant consumerism," with compassion mostly a sideshow. And if we aren't battling materialism, then we've already lost the battle. Humility, the best of all virtues, is also lost as God becomes our errand boy, delivering health and wealth on demand. And with honesty, compassion and humility—no small things in view of Micah 6:8—sacrificed to the so-called "abundant life," this gospel's connection to Jesus grows perilously thin.

Biblically speaking, being open to God's supernatural power isn't enough. Faith must be radically God-centered also, meaning that prayer always seeks God more than his gifts. Otherwise it degenerates into spiritual consumerism, with God as a glorified vending machine. But generous as he is, his ways aren't always our ways. Some of his best gifts look like anything but. Even more than our physical diseases, he wants to free us from the sickness of our souls. And as Psalm 106:15 says, "making" God give you what you want can rob you of what you truly need.

Life can certainly beat us down to the point where we develop a slave mentality, obsessed with scarcity and need. And such negativity undeniably kills the soul. But its opposite, a master mentality, is hardly the solution. C.S. Lewis once observed that errors always come to us in opposing pairs, with each being as bad as the other. Falling from either side of a tightrope is equally deadly. And as Lao Tzu said, "When opposites complement each other everything is in balance."

Wanting success and its fruits is as normal as a newborn's pleasure seeking and pain avoidance. And God really does love to bless and delight his children. Only we must take care lest our stunted desires—even our faith itself—displace the God of the universe in the sanctuary of our hearts.

Sadly, many great and intelligent people have been caught up in some version of prosperity consciousness, but their greatness, intelligence and sincerity prove nothing. Nor do their faith's visible results. Because how could physical wealth and health be more vital than their spiritual counterparts?

The law of attraction does grasp at some very important truths. What we think matters. We can easily act like magnets, bringing on ourselves both good and bad. We aren't mere pawns to be shuffled around the board by unfriendly powers. No, but what we need to see is that our loving God is in control, he's on our side—he loves us—and he hears us when we pray.

The great danger is that the law of attraction can devour everything around it till, minus the gods and goddesses, we've adopted the same paganism the Israelites were tempted by.[2] Because maintaining harmony with the powers that be—whether God or other forces in the universe—while manipulating them for your own ends is nothing new. With one voice, the psalmists and prophets roundly condemned such domestication of prayer as unworthy of the God they served.

To be sure, God does ask us to believe him for the impossible. But biblical faith makes us soldiers in the great war that pits truth against deception. The fight is never about denying reality or displacing absolutely all negative thoughts—a fulltime job if ever there was one! It's about honestly facing reality in the presence of the only One who can redefine it, crying out to him as you obediently walk the faith-walk and doing that no matter how impossible the challenges may seem.

That's what makes Psalm 126 a model for biblical prayer. The psalmist gratefully recounts how sweet and how obviously of God his people's past deliverance was. He asks God to restore their lives and then commits himself to God's law of attraction. That all who honestly walk by faith—despite the hardships and pain— receive his blessing in the end.[3]

There's no denial of reality here and no attempt to manipulate God either. Only honesty, humility and the obedient walking out of faith, despite life's present barrenness. Even though the psalmist's tears are all that water his seeds.

Prayer

Save us, Lord, from all our small-minded efforts to master you. Even in the name of "God-honoring" faith. Far more than anything else we think we need, give us hearts to seek you in spirit and in truth. And despite our weariness and the hardness of the soil, help us believe that you are unfailingly good and will yet turn all our dry rivers into wild torrents of abundance and joy.   Amen.

130

The Love That Will Not Let Me Go

¹From the depths I cry to you, Yahveh.*
²O Lord, hear my S.O.S. and grant your mercy!^a

³If you held onto our sins,* Yahveh
who among us would stand a chance?
⁴But instead you forgive us
and teach us to fear you.

⁵I'm waiting on Yahveh.
Waiting in hope.
Hope in his word.
⁶I long for the Lord
more than a sentry longs for the dawn.
More than a sentry longs for the dawn!
⁷Wait for Yahveh, Israel.*
Because his love for us is unchanged
his redemption as full as ever.
⁸He himself will save us

---

^a From Ernesto Cardenal as quoted by John Goldingay, Tremper Longman III
(ed.), *Psalms, Vol. 3: Psalms 90-150* (Grand Rapids: Baker, 2008) (2008) p. 524.

from all our sins.

I like to think of prayer as a conversation between relative equals, with me always coming at my best to converse with God. But that's precisely what it's not. Infinite in greatness and power, he's infinite in love, justice and humility too. So I can hardly equal him. And since I'm seldom at my best and don't particularly like feeling "less than," seeing my gaping need or asking for help, I don't often *feel* like praying.

This is where the psalmists are so helpful. They see prayer as simply being honest with God. And what would the God of all truth want with some mindless charade where I pretend to be what I'm not, especially when he knows the whole truth about me right from the start? The psalmists see being honest with God as the best way to grow too. To be made whole, we must start by owning our brokenness before him.

So the psalmist here frankly admits she's in dire straits. By not spelling it out beyond that, she allows us to insert our own situation. But she does make one thing clear—and this really comforts me—that whatever her specific trouble is, it relates to her brokenness as a sinner. Whatever other needs she has, her great need is for redemption. All our other needs are really just parts of that whole. Full redemption must address the full extent of our brokenness.

Summing up his time in a Buddhist monastery in California, singer/songwriter Leonard Cohen wrote,

> For many years
> I was known as a Monk
> I shaved my head and wore robes
> and got up very early
> I hated everyone
> But I acted generously

and no one found me out[1]

I love Cohen's honesty. How very tempting to buy into the image we project, but it's never the full story. We may fool others—ourselves even. But we don't fool God. Total authenticity is found only in him.

So the psalmist begins by acknowledging the awful mess she's in. That without God she doesn't stand a chance, can't begin to save herself. But she doesn't tell herself what a bad person she is over and over and over. Instead she focuses on the solution—God her Savior.

I've gone to churches that drilled their members on how consistently they fell short. That assessment may have been fairly accurate of many of us who heard it, but the approach was wrong-headed since it locked us into our sins. Spiritual problems clearly do need diagnosis. But good doctors diagnose in order to empower their patients to get the help they need. Likewise, healthy spiritual diagnosis points us to healing. Why beat people down with blame or shame when, with the psalmist, we can point them to God's mercy, our true hope?

Crying out to him for mercy leads the psalmist to something else none of us can afford to live without—the fear of God.[2] In fact, together these two are the warp and woof of biblical spirituality: undeserved pardon and holy fear.

At first sight they strike us as strange bedfellows. If we fear God rightly, we'll obey him and shouldn't need his forgiveness. On the other hand, if God graciously pardons all our sins, why fear him at all? That is, if he overlooks all the wrongs we do anyway.

But the psalmist has it right. Grace and fear are inseparable. So much so that our grasp of the one is a true measure of our grasp of the other. That's because it's a very specific kind of fear and an equally specific kind of grace. Besides the fear the psalmist speaks of, there's also a bitterly servile fear that knows nothing of

God's grace. It leads us to obey him as a victim obeys a bully. Reluctantly, like we're squeezing the "toothpaste" of our submission out of an almost-empty tube. But the pinched quality of this devotion can't help but depress us and everyone who sees it. So it can hardly bring joy to God.

On the other hand, the nastiness of that fear has led many to preach a cheapened version of grace that abandons the fear of God. It sees God as accepting nearly everyone and everything.[3] Downgrading God's commands to preferences, we end up deciding what's right and wrong for ourselves. In reality though, most of us don't decide for ourselves so much as allow the tide of our culture to carry us wherever it will. And should we take things too far, we trust God will be sympathetic and accept our excuses. So it's all good.

But this works only if we strip God of all moral values, leaving him a wishy-washy character we can't respect, let alone truly love. And since we're called to love him, we're again left eking our devotion out cautiously, sourly. Like we're at the end of our spiritual toothpaste tube and whatever love we give him, he's lucky to get.[4]

If by contrast, he truly hates to see men, women and children degraded for their race, disability, sexual orientation or mental illness, the earth pillaged, the poor oppressed, the homeless forgotten and young girls and boys sold into sexual slavery—if God hates sin—then he doesn't accept everything by a long shot. So the fact that his grace pardons the sins he truly hates makes it anything but cheap.

And being nothing short of stupendous, it calls for a devotion and a discipline that's equally costly. So in the utter hopelessness of our need apart from him and in the magnanimity of his mercy toward us, we discover the fear that's born of love. And this fear of displeasing the God we love actually liberates us since it leads to joyful, exuberant and never grudging devotion.

Our sins, thoughts and actions contrary to God's character and values, inevitably put us where the psalmist finds herself. In dire straits. Which is why we're comforted to know God is in the business of pardoning sin. If he wasn't, none of us would stand a chance. But thankfully, the extent of our rebellion diminishes neither his love for us nor the redemption that flows from it.

Broken and messed up as she is, the psalmist desperately longs for God to come through for her. Knowing he's promised to save her and that his promise is in no wise weakened by his delay, she goes on waiting, trusting, longing.

And she urges us to do the same, assuring us that God will save us from our sins and heal our brokenness. It isn't at the bottom of his To Do list either. Instead he'll have no one else do it on his behalf. He commits *himself* to save us[5]—a fact that's truly staggering in its import.

Prayer

Lord, I'm awestruck to know you've promised to save me, broken as I am. The longer I live, the surer I am it won't happen any other way. Certainly not by my good deeds, a poor amalgam of strength and weakness at best. And since you won't let go of me, I won't let go of you either. So grace me now to live freely and joyfully in the fear that's born of love.   Amen.

131

In God's Arms

[1]My eyes aren't haughty, Yahveh*
nor is my heart arrogant
striving for personal greatness
or things beyond my grasp.

[2]No, I've stilled my soul
like a child on his mother's lap.
Content in her arms.

[3]Wait, Israel, on Yahveh.
Hope in him now and always!

With our marketers charming us non-stop, we all too easily mistake some combination of wealth, status and pleasure for happiness and want a bigger cut of the pie. Never before have so many in our global village had so little and so few had so much, but still we want more. We may finger the rich and famous, yet rank upon rank, we've got this lemming-like fear of being left behind in our mad pursuit of the good life so-called. As writer Charles Yu says, we buy "...things we don't want to feel closer to the things we know we can't get."[1] There are glorious exceptions. But one thing is sure: no one knows contentment nowadays unless they purposely choose it.

In fact, so extreme is our Western approach to self-fulfillment that many feel the need to do, be and have it all. To have successful careers, money, homes, cars, marriage, children, sexual freedom, autonomy, be liberal and green, choose non-conformity, advocate social justice, enjoy urban life, country living, simplicity, fashion, graciousness, good friends, blogging, physical fitness, movies, reading, fine foods and wines, recreational drugs and on and on.

But meeting needs that contradict each other is guaranteed to leave us pulled every which way till the center no longer holds. As social analyst Daniel Yankelovich observes, we aren't "…truly fulfilled by becoming ever more autonomous. Indeed, to move too far in that direction is to risk psychosis, the ultimate form of autonomy."[2]

Even avoiding that, we're still pulled in other ways because pride and egotism are stowaways in all the good we do. In things as commendable as sheltering the homeless or saving the planet, as major as choosing a career or life partner, as mundane as buying clothes or computers. Desiring to be admired as intelligent, talented, kind, dedicated, cool or whatever else we value is normal enough. But it becomes wrong when we let those desires displace what's truly vital.

Why are we like this? Though we're all selfish, the Torah says we weren't created to live this way. The Buddha was quite right to see selfishness at the root of our lostness. But he painted with far too broad a brush when he blamed *all* desire for our drivenness. Because that leaves us no hope except in a deadening escape from ourselves. By contrast, living whole lives means living *passionately* in oneness with God, ourselves, each other and the world around us.

Desiring pleasure, a comfortable, fulfilling life and even greatness isn't necessarily wrong, any more than being seen as good, powerful, talented or cool is. The problem is that our essential oneness with God has been fractured, skewing our desires in the direction of our broken selves. That distortion affects all we do, making an endless range of substandard visions of greatness, pleasure and self-fulfillment seem right. And only God can reveal our blindness to us.

A simple case in point: I once bought some luggage that cost a lot more than I could afford at the time. It was sturdy, lightweight and stylish. Insisting that my family and I deserved the best, I rationalized my choice extensively. But the more I silenced the objections within, the more conflicted I was and the less joy i felt over my new prize.

Ironically just weeks later the new luggage was badly defaced by a shipping company that hadn't remotely heard of customer service. Soon afterwards a banking error beyond our control left us temporarily unable even to buy blankets in a climate far colder than we'd expected. I recall wishing we could somehow crawl inside our empty suitcases for a bit more warmth. They'd served their purpose. But now shorn of their glory, they were just suitcases after all.

My expensive taste wasn't the problem. Beauty, functionality and fine workmanship are all to be prized. But I'd acted without listening to my heart. So the luggage was to me like ill-gotten gain. And that always turns out to be far less than it seems, fueling our lust for "just a little bit more." We'll always have limits of one sort or another. But isn't it better to let our God—who is so much more generous than we are—choose them for us?

In fact a lot of things in life are like that luggage. Clothes, electronics, houses, cars, money, achievements, positions, power, friendships, pleasure, recognition. The thing itself may not be the problem. But entertaining an image of ourselves that dwarfs God, others and the creation around us—an image that disorients us to our true selves and has an insatiable appetite for mere peripherals—certainly is.

Trappist monk Thomas Merton said, "The biggest human temptation is to settle for too little." Too small an idea of self-fulfillment, greatness or joy, as we barter what really matters in life for our overblown dreams. But if we give up all our puny ambitions and desires—what Oswald Chambers once called our "rag rights"—for God's glory, to our utter amazement, we find his dreams for us are far bigger than our own.

What Jewish mother doesn't have bigger dreams for her little boy than he can possibly dream? The psalmist essentially likens God to such a mother. But by contrast, his dreams for us are fully rooted in reality. He knows us truly and still his dreams for us are bigger than we can imagine.

I hear the stripling David singing this psalm before his big face-off with Goliath.[3] Having fled in terror, everyone in Saul's army is utterly baffled by David's unflinching calm. Everyone but his older brothers, that is. They see it as the height of cockiness and angrily accuse him of trying to be a big shot.

They're completely wrong, though. Like a child in his mother's arms, David has nothing to prove. Ignorant of the sweet simplicity he's found in God, his brothers just don't get it. With all ambition surrendered, David is wide open to whatever God wants and nothing else matters. What else explains his unearthly calm?

While David isn't seeking anything lofty for himself, we must also note that it *is* David seeking it. That is, his personality is fully alive in all he does. We mustn't mistake biblical self-surrender for the Eastern concept of self-negation.[4] David clearly submitted his will to God, but he lost neither his personality nor his will in doing so. Instead he sublimated both in the will of God as the repository of true fulfillment, simplicity and rest.

But though true faith and obedience are simple, getting to that place of rest rarely is because accepting God's goals for us involves accepting his means to those ends too. And that's where waiting on him comes in.

Patience is a rare virtue these days. Most of us hate waiting for anything, let alone a God who doesn't necessarily take our calls when we think he should. But partnering with him in the realization of his dreams for us necessitates actively waiting for him to show us what he wants us to be and do—in his time and his way. Without knowing how it's all going to turn out.

It's not like we wait blindfold in the dark. We know realizing God's dreams for us will cost "not less than everything," as T.S. Eliot put it, but also that God's character guarantees the goodness of all we receive from his hand.[5] And for all its challenges, such waiting is still as simple as a little child's lying in her mother's arms, breathing in the peace, freedom and joy she was made for.

So our Buddhist sisters and brothers are right to urgently seek the calm we've all but lost in today's mad world. Only let us seek it, not in self-negation concepts and techniques, but where it's truly found. In God.

Prayer

Your still, small voice rises above the clamor and clang of our world, Lord. Speaking to all that we are, it calls us to freedom and simplicity. All that we long for we find in your outstretched arms. Yet we so often get rattled and rushed, lest the world somehow leave us behind. Center us in you, Lord, that in your holy wisdom, we might know your peace. Amen.

133

Peace Train, Holy Roller

[1]How good and how sweet
when brothers and sisters get along together as one!
[2]It's like the sacred oil
that streamed down the face and beard of Aaron
and on down the collar of his robe.
[3]It's like Hermon's massive dew
descending on Zion's* holy heights.
On such harmony Yahveh* bestows
the blessing of eternal life.

Artfully titled, Tash Aw's novel *The Harmony Silk Factory*[1]
depicts what Jean-Paul Sartre meant when he said, "Hell is other
people." In turn, each of Aw's three narrators make an attempt
at revealing the novel's ultimately unknowable main character.
And it's by their triple failure that Aw delivers his punch, the
sickening awareness that we must all be the same. If we can't know
each other, there can be no trust, love or harmony either. Only
the dark attraction-repulsion of phantoms in an endless cloud of
unknowing.

Few today adopt such out-and-out cynicism, except perhaps
momentarily when overwhelmed by tragedy. Our 13-year-old runs

away to the inner city, our marriage fails or a close friend stabs us in the back. We may use alcohol or some other form of self-medication to keep the lurking beast at bay. But on the surface at least we generally take a more optimistic view of human relations. In fact, many don't believe in human fallenness at all. So even if the reality of our lives tells a darker story—one closer to the media's daily fare—most people today take a generally positive approach to humanity. At least in theory.

The biblical writers' path runs midway between unbridled optimism and cynicism. Glorious as we are, humankind is also fallen. Just as an alcoholic mother's choices shape the life of her fetal alcohol syndrome baby, so the effects of Adam and Eve's disastrous choice are visible in us too. And as unfair as this may seem—since we had no say in the matter—it was only our race's first such blunder. Sin* alienates us not only from God and from ourselves, but from each other and from the creation too. The very first story after our expulsion from Eden has Cain killing his younger brother, Abel.

From there, things spiral downward till God intervenes to stem the tide of violence. While there's judgment in the flood, there's redemption in it too as God commissions Noah's family to mount earth's first "Save the Wildlife" campaign and start over. Later God chooses another family, Abraham's—specifically Isaac's line—to be uniquely his people on earth. He gives them the land of Canaan and later designates Jerusalem as his home among them.

But if the Israelites' alienation from each other is checked somewhat by God's working with them, it remains otherwise unchanged. And so it is with us today. Feeling inadequate in the presence of others, we act badly, take our sister's possessions, undercut our brother's personal gifting or otherwise knock him down. When fear of consequences no longer contains our contempt, we move from covert attacks to open aggression, often enlarged in our brother's response to us.

But with our built-in rationalizers putting the best spin on what we've done 24/7, who has time for guilt? Blinded by our pride, we know what our sister should do far more than what we ourselves should do. And incensed by one thing or another, we move from attack to counterattack, with barely a breath between. And what we do as individuals, we do as families, communities and nations.

Against the universal commonness of such conflict, the psalmist revels in its opposite. Whether between siblings or whole races, as in post-apartheid South Africa, harmony is an astonishingly beautiful thing. Accordingly she gives us two strange but complementary images of it. She first likens it to the scented oil Moses poured on Aaron to anoint him as Israel's* first high priest.[2] No mere perfunctory dab of oil on the forehead so-as-not-to-mess-his-hair, the oil ran down his beard and onto the collar of his robe. Messy as it was, it pictured superabundant empowerment to the ancient Israelites. Overflowing fullness.

The psalmist's second image is even more over-the-top. It's one of dew descending from Lebanon's Mt. Hermon, the region's tallest mountain, onto the heights of Judea. Anyone who who knew both mountains also knew how much of semi-arid Palestine lay between them. So no one would have taken this literally. Some scholars believe the psalm was written after Jerusalem's destruction in 586 BCE, with the name Zion being a pun here, its second meaning being "dry place" or "wasteland."

In any case, the picture is of blessing descending, not only from lofty Hermon, but from beyond Israel's boundaries. So it suggests Zion's central place in God's economy and leads us just where we'd expect a psalm of pilgrimage to lead. To a blessed and fertile Zion at the center of the earth.

Like an ancient version of Yusuf Islam's song "Peace Train," the psalm invited Israelites—whether under Saul, under David,

in the divided kingdom or in the nation returned from exile—
to oneness and peace. Because that was the blessedness
Jerusalem was to be in the earth. Indeed, without the harmony
the psalm pictures, Zion could never be the city *God* was
building.

Sadly, Jerusalem's name, "legacy (or city) of peace," remains
to this day an unfulfilled dream as the city stands for anything
but harmony. In fact, "No piece of ground on the planet is more
contested."³ Evidently God's designation of a people and a city
wasn't enough in itself.

Two other things were needed for Zion to be what God
wanted it to be. The first was his guidance on living peacefully
and the second his supernatural blessing. The psalmist would
have found unity's how-to scattered everywhere throughout the
Tanakh*—the Ten Commandments, Solomon's Proverbs and a
multitude of narrative examples, both good and bad.

But as George Bernard Shaw pointed out, however preferable
peace is to war, it is "infinitely more arduous." Many of the conflicts
we find ourselves in defy simple solutions and require a wisdom
far beyond our own. The Israeli-Palestinian conflict certainly does.
Daniel Pipes says peace is to be found at the end of a gun barrel. If
only his dream was true, we'd all manage nicely. But lasting peace
is found only in justice and dignity for all, in the silence of neither
oppression nor exclusion. And even obeying God's guidance can't
guarantee we'll achieve this lofty goal.

Only his grace and blessing can do that. So we must also
seek him as if our lives depended on it. They do. Peace never
comes from the outside in, but the inside out. The liberality of
a Martin Luther King Jr. or a Nelson Mandela always begins in
God's humble and openhearted generosity to us, as his anointing
empowers us to be ambassadors of his peace.

Only secure in his embrace, can we risk the hostility and
rejection we're bound to encounter *en route*. So we surrender to

God, listen to our hearts and either wait on him or else take the next step—all of which requires truly heroic faith and the rich abundance of God's blessing.

Thankfully, this Zion is of God's own design and building. So how could he not be more committed to our reaching home than we are? And embracing forgiveness and peace, we embrace eternal life itself.

Prayer

Only you, Lord, can free us from our infernos of self-alienation, distrust and abuse and lead us to that holy place where we'll all truly live as one. So teach us your way and descend on us like Hermon's dew. Because however long and hard the way to love and peace is, there's nowhere else to go. Come, Lord, take us home again! Amen.

137

The Jagged Edge of Justice

¹By the rivers of Babylon
we sat and wept over Zion.*
²⁻³Then our captors ordered happy songs
so we hung our lutesᵃ on the poplars.
"Come on now!" they taunted.
"Sing us your favorite Zion song!"
⁴But how could we sing Yahveh's* song
so far away in exile?

⁵If I ever forget you, Jerusalem
may my strumming hand be paralyzed!
⁶May my tongue stick to the roof of my mouth
if I prize anything more than Zion!

⁷Don't ever forget what the Edomites did
at Jerusalem's fall, Yahveh
saying: "Raze it! Right down to its foundations!"

ᵃ Though the word is usually translated "harps," the instrument was far more like
a guitar than a modern-day harp. Hence, my compromise decision to render it
as lutes.

[8]Beautiful brain-bashing Babylon,
a blessing on whoever repays you in kind
for all you did to us!
[9]Yes, blessed be those who wrench your infants
from your arms
and crack their skulls
against the rocks!

A longtime favorite of atheists, this psalm admittedly lends itself to the most honest expressions of hatred. And that's made many Christians consider it "unchristian" and handle it like a hot potato.[1] But while honest prayers are the only prayers God cares for and while "happy" and "lucky" are perfectly good translations of the Hebrew word 'esher in other contexts, we needn't use them here—as if brutality is the psalmist's idea of a good time.[2]

Beyond their bare meaning, words carry an emotional punch and evoke images, positive or negative. Even simple words like "apple pie" can evoke a whole catalog of things from Mom's down-home goodness and teenage innocence to the postwar American dream. In ancient Hebrew, the word 'esher was at least as powerful since God's blessing was so central to Israel's* identity.

That's why to understand the text truly, we must start with the paradigm of covenant reciprocity, of divine blessing and cursing. But let's have no illusions: even read in its fuller context, the psalm is stark and horrifying. It's meant to be. Because nothing less will do justice to the story it recounts.

Reciprocity is just the idea of karma—you reap what you sow—except that here it's carried out by God. Given that God was putting Abraham's family on his team, so to speak, karma is integral to his promise to Abraham in Genesis 12:3—"Whoever blesses you I'll bless and whoever curses you I'll curse." Anyone's treatment of Israel, whether good or bad, resulted in God's treating them in kind.

But reciprocity worked *within* the covenant too. The Israelites were promised blessing if they obeyed God's law and punishment if they rebelled. And as I've noted elsewhere, Yahveh wasn't averse to using others to punish Israel, though he'd eventually punish them for their evil too. This is the psalmist's worldview. After waiting patiently for many long years, God had finally authorized Nebuchadnezzar to overrun Jerusalem. In doing so Nebuchadnezzar brutally slaughtered multitudes and marched multitudes more off to Babylon as slaves.

That's where the psalmist's sad tale is set—ironically, on the banks of the very rivers that furnished primeval Eden's trees with all their abundance. But instead of fullness and joy, the trees now picture their loss. That and goodness's quiet defiance of dehumanizing evil.

That's what I love about the psalm. It would do Rosa Parks proud. Because when the psalmist's abusers ordered him and the others mourning Jerusalem's desolation to sing them a happy, upbeat Zion song, they stonily hung their lutes on the nearby trees. They would not play entertainers to those who laughed in the face of their broken-hearted God, at the joke that Zion had become.

Leaving us to wonder what reprisals their refusal brought on, the psalmist then professes, not blind faith in a merely human city, but rather bold commitment to a city whose smoldering ruins attested to both God's justice and his faithful love for his people.[3] You can't really have one without the other. Far from signaling God's renunciation of either, Zion's fall spoke volumes about his ongoing commitment to both. That's why, though a prisoner in Babylon, the psalmist refuses to give up on Zion and even puts its welfare before his own.

Verse 7 implicitly calls on God to honor his promise to Abraham by treating the Edomites as they'd treated them. Verses

8-9 announce that the same brutality glorious Babylon had inflicted on Jerusalem would be returned to her in due course. And grisly though it is, those who eventually executed God's judgment on Babylon would be blessed in doing so.

The psalm is not saying that God delights in baby bashing. It's talking about justice. The psalmist may well have watched in anguish as his own baby was so bashed to death. Forgive he must because bitterness never destroys its object as much as those who hold it. But forgiveness doesn't eliminate the need for justice. Knowing that justice will one day come to Babylon too enables the psalmist to leave vengeance to God. So the psalm represents a kind of letting go, turning vengeance over to God. And while that isn't forgiveness *per se*, it is vital to it.

For God to be God, he must be just. By making him permissible only insofar as he's "nice," our culture leaves little room for his justice.[4] And that makes the psalm more shocking today than ever.

All this explains our growing interest in the forfeiture of God's personality, the Eastern solution to the problem of compassion versus justice. An *impersonal* law of karma doesn't make life any fairer, but it's somehow less bothersome if justice happens or delays without God's being answerable for it. And that's really what it comes down to: our thinking that God should either answer to us or leave the premises. So besides rethinking our expectations of God—compassion and justice exist only in tension, after all—we must also rethink our right to judge him in the first place.

What do we do with the monstrous evils of Hitler, Stalin and Mao or the Turkish slaughter of Armenians? What do we do with the man who repeatedly rapes his daughter or murders one vulnerable prostitute after another while supposedly leading an upstanding life? What do we say of those who flagrantly destroy earth's endangered species? Is there no need for justice? The psalmist knows there is and that one day God's justice will see every dark, inhuman deed repaid in full. We needn't apologize for this, even if we're the ones violated. Because again, true compassion doesn't exist without justice.

In an age when many dismiss moral absolutes altogether, this psalm's stark honesty is frankly embarrassing. That's another reason we choose the niceness of insipidly positive thinking and the glib superficiality of culturally mandated happiness over the psalmist's pain-wracked lament. But we must distinguish between Disneyesque niceness and true compassion. Because while God weeps over every baby murdered, he also promises that every wrong will be righted in our very imperfect world.

Battered and bruised though he is, the psalmist refuses the Babylonian mockery of God and of life in general. Like Martin Luther King Jr. in the middle of the civil rights campaign, he commits with renewed zeal to Zion's undying future. Because even in Babylon he dreams of the justice God has committed himself to. Affirming its unshaken reality in God, the psalmist calls for it to be executed. And he implicitly calls us to hope in God's faithfulness and join him in faith's daring resistance of evil.

Prayer

I don't like seeing brokenness or pain, Lord. But you'd have me weep with those who weep—not pretend things are fine when they aren't. Help me to see that compassion can't exist without justice, to take justice on your terms and to live for Zion, the civilization you're building on earth.   Amen.

139

The Anatomy of Hate

¹Yahveh,* you've searched me and know me inside out.
²Know when I stand up and sit down
understand my thoughts before I think them.
³Whether I stay in or go out
you comprehend all I do.
⁴Before I utter a word, Yahveh
you know what I'm going to say.
⁵I go forward, you're there.
Backward, there too…
with your hand resting on me!
⁶I can't begin to grasp this—
it's way over my head.

⁷Where could I run from your spirit?
Where escape from your presence?
⁸If I soared into the heavens you'd be there
and if I bedded down in the underworld
you'd be there too, Yahveh.
⁹If I took the wings of the morning
and flew off to the ends of the earth
¹⁰even there your hand would guide me

and hold me tight.
[11]And if I said, "The dark of night will hide me"
it would do no such thing
because darkness isn't dark to you
[12]hides nothing from you.
To you night is just like day—
dark or light makes no difference at all.

[13]You created my most obscure parts
wove me together in my mother's womb.
[14]I praise you for making me
so intricate, miraculous, unique.
[15]Nothing was hid from you
when sperm and egg united in secret[a]
and I was knitted together
deep inside my mother's womb.[b]
[16]Seeing my shapeless form
you marked out all my days
missing nothing from start to finish
before I even breathed my first.
[17]How astonishing your thoughts to me—
how incalculable, God!
[18]If I could count them
they'd outnumber earth's grains of sands—
and if I ever finished counting them
I'd be as great as you.

[19]If only you'd kill the wicked, God—

---

[a] The text says simply, "…when I was made in secret…"
[b] Literally, "in the depths of the earth." To heighten the mystery of conception, the psalmist refers to the womb metonymically as the earth it came from (Gen. 2:7).

get away from me, you gangsters!^{c}
^{20}They work you into their schemes.
Your enemies use your name
for their own futile designs.
^{21}How I hate those who hate you, Yahveh
and loathe those who oppose you!
^{22}I count all your enemies my own
and feel nothing but hatred for them.
^{23}Examine me, Yahveh—probe my every thought.
^{24}See if I've chosen any wayward paths
and lead me in your eternal way.

Vancouver is a long way from Kansas. But not to the pastor of Topeka's hatemongering Westboro Baptist Church. In 2008 he threatened to picket a Vancouver production of *The Laramie Project*, a play about the 1998 murder of Wyoming gay college student Matthew Shepherd.

Locked in their anti-gay ideology, Westboro's members picketed Shepherd's funeral with signs saying "Matthew Shepherd Rots in Hell" and "God Hates Fags." Since then they've demonstrated at numerous events—many related to homosexuality only in their twisted logic—making nothing clearer than how much they thrive on negative publicity.

Thankfully, Canadian border guards ensured that no one from Kansas picketed in Vancouver. Even better, the churches of East Vancouver joined forces in a rally in support of *The Laramie Project*. Because by showing contempt for the murdered gay student, Westboro's members were actually on the wrong side of the line drawn by Psalm 139, a passage they mistakenly base their hate on.

---

^{c} Literally, "men of blood."

Verses 19-20 are key to understanding the psalmist. He describes those he abhors as religious thugs. One translation says, they "...invoke You for intrigue..."[1] In other words, they claim God wants them to carry out their violent, self-centered acts. And verse 20 concludes: they "use your name for their own futile designs."[2] So the psalmist hates those who try to make God the godfather behind their violence and abuse.

Who besides Westboro's picketers fit the psalm's description? Islamist recruiters who seduce depressed Muslim youth into running suicide missions for them. And with them, Catholic priests who sexually abuse young boys, swearing them to secrecy in God's name. Fundamentalist Christians who murder abortionist doctors or burn the scriptures of others. And every religious leader who manipulates people into silencing questions, honest doubts and conscience too.

Anyone can do evil in God's name, convince himself that since he's "on God's side," his actions invariably please God. But saying it—even sincerely believing it—doesn't make it true. Such empty use of God's name is the very thing the Ten Commandments forbid. Far worse than cursing or using God's name disrespectfully is doing evil under a cloak of pretended spirituality. In God's name. This is the height of egofaith.

This relates to another of religion's great dangers: the ease with which power-hungry manipulators use it to turn sincere people—whole congregations—into battalions of foot soldiers, mere fodder for their machine. Nothing is more vital to their self-serving enterprise than the sort of divine namedropping by which they stamp all their misguided empire building—including abuse and violence God has no part in—with his imprimatur.

Wrong as Westboro is, though, the antidote to such hatemongering is not the rejection of all hate. Despite its being one of the pillars of our tolerant society, this too is wrong. Hate is a normal reaction to whatever we absolutely reject. And as such, it's as vital to our humanity as love. We can restrict ourselves to diminutives like "can't stand" or "have no use for" if we want. But the fact is, we all feel hatred at times and are no better for pretending we don't.[3]

Perhaps the role of hatred in great drama can help us here. *Shawshank Redemption* (1994), *The Matrix* (1999) and *The Princess Bride* (1987) are among my all-time movie favorites. As different as they are, they all present a clear picture of evil, including characters we're meant to hate. We've only to hear Shawshank's warden welcome new inmates to instinctively loathe him: "I believe in two things: discipline and the Bible. Here you'll receive both. Put your trust in the Lord; your ass belongs to me. Welcome to Shawshank."[4]

The villains in all three stories are as contemptuous as they are powerful. *The Matrix*'s bloodless Agent Smith, for example, with his "I'm going to enjoy watching you die, Mr. Anderson."[5] But each story's tension is finally resolved through good's triumphing over evil. Not only does Neo Anderson stop Agent Smith's bullets in mid-air. He also "appropriates" him, making his physical shell explode in a sea of code. And when he does, we shout "Yes!" And so we should. Anyone given to cruelty and oppression to the extent that Agent Smith is, clearly deserves our hatred.

Many Christians struggle with this. They mistakenly think Jesus' command to "love your enemies" leaves no room for hatred.[6] By contrast, Jewish readers are typically more matter-of-fact and, really, more honest in their acceptance of the psalmist's hatred. Biblically speaking, it's the *kind* of hate we allow and what we *do* with it that's critical. Oxymoron though it may seem, we need to cultivate healthy hatred.[7]

The psalmist begins with a reverie of God's greatness and the intimacy of his relationship to him. He acknowledges that God knows him inside out,[8] has got the whole world in his hand and lovingly shaped his entire life before he was even born.[9]

And overwhelmed by God's loving and sovereign commitment to him, he makes a similarly extravagant return commitment to God.[10]

He hates these gangsters whose religion is as anti-God as it gets. But he doesn't spit on them, burn their holy book or otherwise abuse them. That's what God's enemies do. God's friends pour out their anger to him in prayer. They choose to walk in his way, pray he'll rid the earth of *his* enemies and beg him to search them for any sign that they're slipping into their evil ways.

Prayer

Thank-you for loving me as you do, Lord. Help me to hate those who turn faith into contempt for those you cherish most—namely, the least of our brothers and sisters. And help me give my hatred for those who abuse the weak and vulnerable in your holy name to you. Search me and keep me from all their evil, I pray. Amen.

146

Wings

[1]Praise Yahveh* everyone—myself included!
Praise Yahveh!
[2]I will praise him as long as I live
sing praise to God with my very last breath.

[3]Don't put your faith in high-powered leaders—
mere mortals who all prove helpless in the end.
[4]When they breathe their last, they're dead and gone
and all their big plans with them.
[5]But those who turn to Jacob's God are blessed,
who hope in Yahveh,
[6]Maker of earth, sea, sky and everything in them.

As the keeper of his word forever
[7]Yahveh gives justice to the oppressed
and feeds the hungry.
Yahveh sets captives free, [8]opens blind eyes
and lifts up the burdened.
He loves those who do right
[9]protects outsiders and empowers orphans and widows
but he brings evildoers* to ruin.

[10]Yahveh will reign forever!
Yes, your God, Zion,* will reign for all time!
Praise Yahveh!

The psalmists frequently urge—even command—us to praise God, something many find bothersome. "What kind of God demands our praise?" they object. "Is Yahveh so insecure that he can't be happy unless we're stroking his ego non-stop?"

No one speaks to this more persuasively than one-time skeptic C.S. Lewis in his *Reflections on the Psalms*. Lewis was thrown by it until three things occurred to him about the nature of praise. The first is that praise is normal to human life. He writes: "...the most obvious fact about praise—whether of God or anything— strangely escaped me... I had never noticed that all enjoyment spontaneously overflows in praise..."[1]

Shyness or the fear of boring others may sometimes check our praise. But not usually. Says Lewis, "The world rings with praise..." Lovers praise each other, players their chosen game, fans their favorite athlete, hikers the awesome view. We praise great beer, food, cars, clothes, movies, music, architecture, technology, weather, animals, children, politicians and thinkers. Enjoyment leads naturally to praise.[2]

Lewis's second realization was that praise is almost "inner health made audible." He writes that he hadn't noticed "how the humblest, and at the same time most balanced and capacious, minds, praised most, while the cranks, misfits and malcontents praised least..." To not praise what we value suggests a fear of diminishing our own worth by praising another.[3]

And last but not least, Lewis realized that praise is itself integral to our enjoyment. He says he hadn't noticed either that "just as [people] spontaneously praise whatever they value, so they spontaneously urge us to join them in praising it..." Isn't that beautiful? ...incredible? ...amazing? we ask. So in urging us to praise God, the psalmists are doing only what we all do when we talk about anything we value.

Lewis continues:

>…My whole, more general, difficulty about the praise of God depended on my absurdly denying to us, as regards the supremely Valuable, what we delight to do, indeed what we can't help doing, about everything else we value.
>
>I think we delight to praise what we enjoy because the praise not merely expresses but completes the enjoyment; it is its appointed consummation. It is not out of compliment that lovers keep on telling one another how beautiful they are; the delight is incomplete till it is expressed.[4]

The Westminster Catechism says humankind's chief end is "to glorify God and enjoy him forever." And Lewis concludes that "…these are the same thing. Fully to enjoy is to glorify. In commanding us to glorify Him, God is inviting us to enjoy Him."[5]

Since we were created for relationship with God, every act of praise we offer him fulfills us. Far from being an imposition on us, God's call to worship is just like a songbird's urging its young to sing.

In one sense, doing anything God asks of us is worship. But since both language and music are definitive of who we are, it only makes sense that singing is central to our worship. We worship in music, word and body language that together express our hearts.

We do this to the best of our ability but without letting our desire for technical correctness divert our attention from God. Because while worship disconnected from the heart may fool us who engage in it, such self-focused performances never fool God.

Not that we should be too hard on ourselves though. Nothing we ever do is perfect. And true worship is about learning to give ourselves without reservation. Finding ourselves as we lose ourselves in God. Something perhaps like a baby bird's learning to fly.

Thankfully we pour out our hearts in praise and devotion not before some cold and silent deity, but a God who meets us in our worship and whose love both precedes and follows ours. Our self-giving is simply the reply to his self-giving to us. Which makes all our worship dialog, both dynamic and interactive. So how could God's requiring it be small-minded when it's his invitation to love?

Whether we laugh and dance or weep and lament, worship has a way of transforming us too. As we see his beauty, his perfect likeness—warped and distorted in us since the fall—is restored in us. And in that sense philosopher Ralph Waldo Emerson is right in saying that "…what we are worshipping we are becoming." So even kneeling with our faces to the ground, worshipping God never degrades or diminishes. It always lifts and enlarges.

It's not that God needs our worship. His call to worship is an invitation to truth and the freedom it brings. A call to something quintessentially human, raised to a level all its own. So why should we care if God seeks his own glory when the worship he requires is for our good?

Seeing high-powered celebrities in sports, entertainment, business or politics, we're often impressed. But the psalmist reminds us that all their strength and glory is eventually spent. All their plans buried with them.

Our trust must ultimately be in God, whose power is endless. He is also unfailingly trustworthy. He sides with the widow, orphan and oppressed. And he doesn't just offer some wan smile from afar. No, he acts on behalf of the marginalized—feeding, releasing, healing, lifting, defending. He also judges evildoers. All this characterizes his endless reign and this is what the psalmist invites us to celebrate.

The imperfections of our world are everywhere painfully

visible. We now witness homelessness with routine familiarity, for example. There are likely as many reasons for it as there are homeless people. This week's *Vancouver Sun* told one woman's story, of vicious childhood sexual abuse pushing her into drugs, which then catapulted her into mental illness. Other cases are the product of lost jobs, family breakdown, serious injury or decline in health.[5] Still others of corporate greed and government negligence combined with our rampant consumerism. God often doesn't intervene as we'd like him to.

But if we start with the world's brokenness and view everything—God included—through it, we end in despair. Because being warped and misshapen, this lens distorts everything, making God the problem. The alternative is to begin as the psalmist does, with God's impeccable character, and view the world through that lens—with hope.

In an age that "...idolizes appraisal but is uncomfortable with praise..." Kathleen Norris says, the psalmists enable us to see "... that praise does not spring from a delusion that things are better than they are, but rather from the human capacity for hope and joy."[6] Praise helps the psalmist see God's compassion and justice, despite the evil around her.

Starting with God's goodness, power and faithfulness, she calls us to worship. Our worship pleases God. And because we were made to know him, it also fulfills us perfectly, restoring his likeness in us—making us more just, compassionate and humble in all we do.

Prayer

Knowing who you are, Lord, how can I help but bow in adoration, weep tears of gratitude and sing for joy? Grant me your grace that, in company with your people, I might give you all that I am—body, mind and heart. Reveal your matchless beauty both to me and through me. Give me wings to fly! Amen.

150

Unending Song

[1]Hallelujah![a]
Praise God in his temple here below.
Praise him in the vast expanse of his heavens above.
[2]Praise him for his acts of power.
Praise him for his infinite greatness.

[3]Praise him with trumpet fanfare
praise him with piano and violin crescendo
[4]praise him with tambourines and dancing
praise him with guitar and flute
[5]praise him with the sizzle of cymbals
praise him with an almighty crash of cymbals!
[6]Let everything that lives and breathes praise Yahveh.*
Hallelujah!

Wilfred Cantwell Smith once asked a group of Muslim students what they considered their faith's single greatest cultural expression. After conferring together they replied with evident satisfaction, "The Taj Mahal." And what a magnificent choice!

---

[a] *Hallelujah* means "Praise Yahveh!"

When the students threw the question back at Smith, asking for Christianity's equivalent, his answer stunned them. It was Handel's *Messiah*, best known for its rousing "Hallelujah Chorus." It would never have occurred to them to choose a musical creation. Because for all its greatness in so many other respects, the Islamic faith tragically forbids music in all its "orthodox" forms of worship.[1]

But as the Psalms so clearly attest, worship and song go hand in hand, biblically speaking. And that's why this psalm—the last of the book's five concluding psalms—is so fitting an ending to the book. G.B. Caird says "...a doxology is by its very nature both an affirmation and a call to worship."[2] And while doxology is found throughout these psalms, the psalmist clearly means here to pull out all the stops and present this last affirmation and call with a gusto that's unmistakable even without the musical score.

The call to worship in ancient Israel was always addressed to the whole person—emotions, no less than body and mind. So as we've seen before, the Psalms tell us to sing and shout for joy—something we do at football stadiums and public events, celebrating far lesser objects. Yet many think we should only halfway celebrate the greatest object of worship in existence, maintaining our dignity at all times. Bringing in loud percussion and dance, the psalmist clearly disagrees. Not that worship must be lively or loud to qualify. No, but lively and loud do qualify too.

Our false modesty is nothing new. When King David danced before the Lord, his wife Michal was horrified that he'd made himself so ordinary, so plebian, before his subjects.[3] But David knew that before Yahveh, we're all commoners and that he demands of us all that we are.

Even without mentioning the word, Psalm 150 is all about joy. Because celebration apart from joy is mere formality—hardly what the psalmist means to inspire here.

However happily we celebrate the land of our birth, the celebration of God goes far beyond national celebrations. For starters, he has neither beginning nor end. And his love and justice never fail or fall short. We all know great people whose greatness is *mostly* matched by their humility. But God's greatness is infinite and his humility matches it perfectly.

We also celebrate the great things God has done for us and what they say about him. His love is passionate, as welcoming to the humble as it is inaccessible to the arrogant. Nothing about him is passive. He always acts on our behalf, even if it means actively awaiting our response. And he is more father and mother than the very best of their earthly kind. So why shouldn't we celebrate him?

But we only celebrate what we have eyes to see. Novelist Marilynne Robinson writes of being aware in childhood of God as "…a vast energy of intention, all around me, barely restrained." So obvious was this to her that she thought everyone else must be aware of it too.[4]

I've known a few adults with a similar awareness of God, but only a few. I must confess I'm often unmindful of the God I live and move and have my being in. And just as our gestures automatically diminish in size when we're in a confined space, so I live smaller as a result. Living large means living in all the breadth and width, the height and depth of God's love. What could possibly be bigger? Some days I'm more aware than others, but getting caught up in the small stuff, I often lose sight of the big picture.

We say "perception is reality" and in a very real sense it's true. Josef Albers says of color perception, "What counts here— first and last—is not so-called knowledge of so-called facts, but vision—seeing."[5] Imagination takes a medium tone that looks light next to black and makes it look dark next to white. What we bring to a landscape or painting by way of imagination trumps the actual facts of its color composition in importance.

We could say the same thing of spiritual sight. Not that God is a mere figment of imagination. The psalmist would never brook such a thought. We know who God is by what he does. And he acts both powerfully and visibly in history. But still to truly see him requires a certain kind of sight.

When Yahveh freed the Israelites from slavery, Pharaoh saw only an upstart god as power-hungry as he was. The picture we have of God—whether scoundrel, weakling, dictator or friend —strongly colors whatever we see of him. Seeing him without the distortions of our minds interfering, means being enlarged in the process. It's what centers us and frees us to know the joy he made us for.

This will sometimes give us the look of a young André Agassi stepping out on the court to win. The image in his mind registers in his expression and bearing and ultimately in his effectiveness on the court. In our times of anguish, it will have an entirely different look. Maybe something like the dying Jesus. Partier that he was, he wore no smile in death. But even in his darkest hour, he lived life large because he lived it in God, centered in him.

It's safe to say that no amount of imagination can give Agassi his Wimbledon-winning forehand back now. Change and decay are in all we see. But joy isn't so much about the molecular composition of our colors as it is how we see our lives. Seeing them in God infuses the dullest grays and the blackest blacks with fire and light. Even the anguish of a Psalm 22 or 137 is backlit with joy in the God who is its larger context. So the compiler(s) of the Psalms chose this psalm—brimming with joy in the God who is our life—to bring the great collection to its summation.

Like us, the psalmists doubtless strained to see what lay beyond this life. Making this final psalm about joy in God, the book implicitly points beyond. But any idea of Paradise that gets stuck in its physical aspects—pearly gates, golden streets—is hardly worth the name. Heaven is the perfection of joy precisely because it's the fullness of God.

On that day we won't need the psalmists to call us to worship because we'll see God with perfect clarity. But here, amid life's many distractions, her affirmation and call helps us refocus, center ourselves again in God and rejoin each day anew the Hallelujah Chorus that will never end.

Prayer

Taken up with all my little concerns, I become small as a result and then project my smallness onto you. No one but you can open my eyes to see you as you are, Lord. Touch my eyes then and help me see. Help me live large in you, my whole life a celebration of the joy that you are both now and always. Amen.

Outro

Ancient Psalms for Today

As faith-wracked as our generation is, two of my premises are that we're all believers by design and that the Psalms can help us recover our faith in God like nothing else. There are three reasons why they do this.

First, they introduce us to ordinary people who found their trust in God challenged just as ours is today by a veritable circus of misdirected faith. There were two big acts in that circus. The first was Canaanite religion's mix-n-match extravaganza, offering the immediacy of religious sex rites and idolatry, along with a promise of freedom. Specifically, the freedom to do pretty much as you pleased morally and supplement your religion with magic or whatever else wherever it was found wanting.

But as with its pagan and New Age equivalents today, Canaanite religion's freedom was illusory. Because too many choices—whether moral or faith choices—turns out to be murky, confusing, more burden than blessing. And while every faith system encourages loyalties of one kind or another, the only one that was utterly forbidden by Canaanite religion was faith in Yahveh.*

Had Canaanite religion been the only challenge the psalmists were up against, things wouldn't have looked so bleak. But most of the attacks on them came from fellow Israelites who professed the selfsame faith in God. King Saul—together with the entire community that supported him—worshipped Yahveh just as David did. But they gave themselves to oppression and they did so in God's name. This was the second act in the circus of unbelief confronting the psalmists.

But oppressive faith in God is a contradiction in terms since he simply isn't like that. So their religion became a magic show second to none While Yahveh figured large in Saul's religion, he turned out to be just the girl in the box getting all the swords run through her. A mere prop in the show. Not the magician. That would be Saul. And oppressive monotheism today—whether Christian, Jewish or Muslim—still tries to use God like that to authorize its ungodly mix of egofaith and evil.

So today we have the New Age and Neopagan movements on the one hand, and on the other hand, various strains of oppressive religion. In that sense, while almost everything is different from the ancient world, how much has really changed?

Against all that, the psalmists spoke of a God who demands our absolute devotion and who sides with the oppressed against their oppressors—a God of mercy and justice. As their psalms make plain, they were convinced that no mere god could possibly be worthy of that kind of devotion.

The second reason the psalms are so good at helping us recover faith in the midst of unbelief is to be found in their back story. The Psalms don't just tell us about good men and women who expressed their faith in God in song. All three monotheistic faith communities have gone on record as saying that the Book of Psalms was given by God—inspired by him. We differ specifically on how we believe that happened. But we all agree that they were given by God. So the back story here is that God is reaching out to us in love, drawing us to himself.

One of the key ways he does that is by embracing our full

humanity. As we've seen, the faith he has the psalmists model for us isn't always "nice" or even "polite." Whenever religion is incessantly nice or proper it becomes insipid, disconnected from God, who clearly isn't always nice or proper. Disconnected from God. Rather, by their truth telling, the Psalms keep us from perverting the more disturbing aspects of God's character into something selfish and unholy. So the faith he asks of us is full-blown, matching the whole of both who God is and who we were made to be. And that gives it the ring of truth.

The third reason the Psalms help us recover faith is that they're so experiential. This isn't a book of rules or even stories, as vital as those are in scripture. It's a book of songs we sing or pray back to God in response to his overtures to us in the very psalms we pray. Poetry—and song in particular—touches the heart in ways few other things do. So our faith is strengthened as we respond by opening our hearts to his warm embrace.

Talking about God and faith can be eminently worthwhile. But even that goes only so far. The main thing is to love God as he loved us in redeeming us and giving us the Psalms. One key way we do that is through prayer and worship, sharing our lives with him. So each of these songs becomes an expression of our love for him even as it expresses his love for us. And that's one thing that gives the Psalms their staying power.

Making the Psalmists' Spirituality Ours

My goal here has been to give some sense of the spirituality of the Psalms, relating it as faithfully as possible to our time and place. But two constraints I've worked under have left me feeling like I've only scratched the surface. The first is that I've done only 40 psalms, leaving the great majority—110 of them—undone.

The second is that I've limited myself to the Psalms. It's been challenging to speak of a single book of scripture without being able to adequately put it in its larger context in the Tanakh* or Hebrew Bible. This inevitably leaves many questions unanswered, many ends loose. But presenting the spirituality of the entire Tanakh accurately and faithfully is for another day, another book.

My prayer in writing is that my readers will see God's heart for them in the Psalms, that however weak or unworthy they feel, they'll remember that he loves them and wants to welcome them home. He longs for us to know him and be remade in that knowledge. He wants us to come as we are. Best of all, he cares not just about us as individuals, but about the health and healing of our world.

As ancient as these prayer songs are, we make them ours by praying them heart and soul. If reading this book helps any of my readers to do that, I will be well satisfied.

Beyond the Psalms

The psalms are starter prayers, lessons on prayer, designed to inform and complement our own praying. So another goal I've had in writing has been to prompt my readers to write their own prayers, whether in visible texts they can share with others or simply inscribed on their hearts in the intimacy of their times alone with God.

The challenge is for us to make the psalms our own in the sense that the great composers made all the masterpieces they studied their own. They did this not just by reproducing them faithfully, but by going beyond them too. Because the new music they composed simultaneously expressed their uniqueness as individuals as well as how the compositions of all their teachers had shaped them into who they'd become. So we might say that they "composed" their predecessors' compositions into something fresh and new, but at once equally old and rich.

That's what the psalmists did too, composting the prayers of Abraham, Jacob, Moses, Miriam, Deborah, Hannah, Job and all the other ordinary spiritual greats who had gone before them.

As challenging as it is, this is the essence of true spirituality, what makes it dynamic, unique to each of us and yet thoroughly infused with the life of God. He doesn't want us to have a second-hand relationship with him. No, but far from insulating us from God, the psalmists take us to him. Giving the brokenness they see in themselves and in the world around them to God in prayer, they take us with them into the very heart of God. By praying their prayers, we both change our world and learn to love as God loves. And that unquestionably puts the Psalms at the heart of God's great universal invitation to love and to life.

Glossary

atone   To take action that will heal a broken
relationship—first and foremost, with God—
and win the offended party's blessing.
Atonement is inextricably linked with animal
sacrifice, which goes back to the first family,
with Abel's fateful offering in Genesis 4. But the
language and legal requirements of sacrificial
atonement were given to Moses at Sinai.
Interestingly, Psalm 65:3 says God will atone for
our sins.

covenant   God made a variety of covenants with his people
throughout biblical history, the one he
established through Moses at Mount Sinai acting
like Israel's constitution. By it, God committed
himself to care for the Israelites as *their* God and
they to obey him as *his* people. The Torah
represents that covenant in scriptural form.

evildoers   The Tanakh presents two groups of people,
morally speaking: those who love and obey God
and those who disregard him and his laws,
choosing evil instead. The former are called
righteous because God's grace empowers them
to do right. The latter not only disobey God,
they also spurn the offer of his free grace.

Israel Meaning "Prince with God," Israel refers to both Jacob and the nation that came from him. In giving Jacob this name, God promised him the nobility, authority and richness of his own divine character (Gen. 32). The fact that Jacob's family went by this name meant that they shared both his moral deficiency and God's gracious promise to remedy it.

Messiah While the Hebrew word literally refers simply to someone "anointed" to rule, it took on an entire profile during David's lifetime. This was when it came to mean the promised ideal king who is both David's descendant and heir to all the promises God gave him concerning the restoration of his perfect rule on earth.

the nations All the ethnic peoples—including the states and empires they grew into—who opposed God's covenant with Israel as Egypt did in Moses' day. The nations were given to idolatry as well as a multiplicity of gods and these proved a constant temptation to the ancient Israelites. So the nations threatened Israel both militarily and spiritually.

the poor While we typically define poverty in terms of finances, the biblical writers use the term to cover anyone marginalized by an oppressor, as David was by King Saul. Such oppression invariably has monetary consequences that leave its victims vulnerable in many ways. Hence, the word includes refugees, widows, orphans, etc. While the biblical record shows poverty resulting from laziness and folly also, its focus is on the many poor most people don't see: namely victims of oppression.

sacrifice The sacrificial offering of sheep, goats, bulls, pigeons and other animals can be traced back to Abraham and beyond. It was a central part of Israel's covenant revealed to Moses. There were also offerings of oil and grain. All of these offerings were meant to be as tangible expressions of repentance for sin and faith in God's redemption—and were often coupled with urgent prayer and thanksgiving or praise for his goodness and grace.

sin Sin includes all actions, thoughts and omissions that violate God's covenant of love, whether we're aware that they do or not. Being blind to my arrogance, for example, doesn't change the fact that I'm being arrogant. To reject God's character—spelled out in terms of justice, humility and compassion—is to violate his covenant.

Tanakh The Jewish scriptures, which make up the part of the Bible Christians call the Old Testament. By contrast, the Qur'an refers to the various components of the Tanakh—e.g. the Zabūr (Psalms). While Jews and Christians arrange the Tanakh/Old Testament somewhat differently, they both include the same books and hold them in much the same reverence.

Torah

Literally "instruction" or "law," the Torah refers to God's blueprint for a balanced, whole and just society as revealed in the opening books of scripture, Genesis through Deuteronomy. While it's often called the Law, one has only to read a few chapters into it—e.g. Genesis 1-3—to see that it's by no means all law *per se*. It doubtless came to be known as the Law due to the fact that God's law was at its core.

Yahveh

According to Exodus 3, God withheld this, his personal name, until he called Moses to rescue the Israelites from Egyptian bondage. With the Hebrew verb *to be* as its root, it means: the self-existent One, the Source of all being, the One who defines us and every situation we face.

Zion

Yahveh chose this small mountain for his earthly home, commanding his people to worship him there. So David built his capital and Solomon his magnificent temple there. But Zion is far more than a geographic location, city or sacred site. It is also the ideal to which God calls his people, the civilization *he* promises to establish, where truth and justice will reign. So the Zionist movement that grew up in 19th century Europe has only formal connections to the Zion extolled by the psalmists.

Notes

Intro

[1] Quranic Arabic for Psalms is *Zabūr*, probably related to the Hebrew *Zamīr* (song). The other relevant Hebrew words are *Mizmôr* (melody) and *Tehillîm* (praises). The English word for Psalms comes from the Greek *Psalmoi*, meaning songs sung to the accompaniment of a harp, the ancient equivalent of our guitar.

[2] *Brother to a Dragonfly* (New York: Continuum, 2000) p. 91.

[3] The name Yahveh (pronounced <u>Yah</u>-vay) was familiar to the Psalms' first readers. Since it is unfamiliar to most readers today, I've included it in my glossary (p. 264).

[4] See pages 11-12 on my use of gender-specific pronouns with reference to God.

[5] Gen. 12:3.

[6] Most Middle Eastern cultures are extremely male chauvinistic to this day and ancient Hebrew culture was certainly no less so. So in paraphrasing general personal references, which in ancient Hebrew called for male nouns and pronouns (e.g. "man" and "he" in Psalm 1) I've chosen to make them all gender neutral. My reason for doing so is that God's purpose was never to endorse such chauvinism, but rather to embrace the Hebrews despite the very real imperfections of their culture.

John Calvin said that in revealing himself to us, God graciously spoke "baby talk" to us. That is, he stooped down to our level to communicate his truth through the limitations of a very imperfect language and culture, so that we could understand. I know such a defense will anger some of my readers, but God had to begin with the human race somewhere. Had he determined to wait till he found a culture that conformed to his values perfectly before revealing his truth to us, we'd all be waiting still.

[7] *Thoughts on Religion and Other Subjects* (New York: Washington Square Press, 1965) p. 271.

[8] Deut. 4:29 and Jer. 29:13.

[9] Deut. 6:5.

[10] In their present form, the Psalms were compiled after Israel's exile to Babylon in 586 BCE and grouped into five books, making them the worshipper's equivalent

to the five books of the Law. We know little about the person (or persons) who compiled them, besides the obvious fact that he was (or they were) devoted to God and his worship in the Psalms.

Mark D. Futato gives a helpful explanation of the Psalms' five-book arrangement in *Interpreting the Psalms: An Exegetical Handbook* (Grand Rapids: Kregel, 2007) pp. 72-116. Psalms 1 and 2 are introductory to all the books that follow, presenting David as the person who is blessed (1), while the nations will be blessed only if they submit to God and David's appointed heir (2). Futato then shows how Books I-II teach that God (partially) fulfilled the promise in David and in Solomon, while Book III has him abandoning his promise in kingless, post-exilic Judah. Book IV says God is king, despite there being no Davidic king, while Book V looks forward to the ultimate fulfillment of the promise in the Messiah, urging us to live by faith, with both hope for the future now and joyful praise always.

The books are divided as follows: I is comprised of Psalms 1-41, II of 42-72, III of 73-89, IV of 90-106 and V of 107-150. Just as Psalms 1-2 introduce the whole, the last 5 psalms (146-50) conclude the whole with a resounding crescendo of praise.

[11] The very same can be said of the Christian community. By contrast, the Muslim community is less confident here. Muslims typically affirm that the Psalms were originally inspired by God, but also allege that the book has long since been corrupted. While they offer no historical evidence to support their allegation, it is vital to their explanations of the discrepancies between the Psalms and their scripture, *The Glorious Qur'an.*

[12] Quoted by Kathleen Norris in *The Cloister Walk* (New York: Riverhead, 1997) p. 91.

[13] *The Message: The Bible in Contemporary Language* (Colorado Springs: Navpress, 2002) pp. 910-11.

[14] More precisely, the psalms are prayer songs meant to be sung to God. Kathleen Norris experienced their power as a member of a Benedictine abbey which sings through the entire book of Psalms every month. For more on this, see *The Cloister Walk.*

[15] While most scholars transliterate YHVH or YHWH as "Yahweh," I hold to Raymond Dillard's view (expressed in a lecture at Westminster Theological Seminary, Philadelphia, PA, in 1982) that "Yahweh" sounds both insipid and un-Jewish and opt here for the more authentic sounding "Yahveh."

[16] To any Jewish readers offended by my use of this name, I sincerely apologize. But while I deeply appreciate the respect Jewish tradition shows for this name, I fear more the loss of intimacy that non-vocalization of it risks. Frankly, I don't see why we should avoid writing Yahveh when Moses and the psalmists were clearly happy to do so. That is, I do in English only what the original text does in Hebrew.

According to Exodus 3:13-15 God revealed this, his personal name, not to Abraham, Isaac or Jacob, but to Moses. With the Hebrew verb *to be* as its root, Yahveh means "the God who defines us and every situation we face."

Most Christian readers will be familiar with this name in its late mistaken form (ca.1100 CE) of "Jehovah." Most Muslims will not be familiar with it at all. In any case, Yahveh is the Hebrew name for the God of Abraham, Moses and David — of Jews, Christians and Muslims. Having said that, however, we must acknowledge that God clearly has many names and move beyond any notion that his *real* name is the one he's called by in our language.

[17] Yahveh may be translated "Self-Existing One" or "Sovereign Lord." To Muslims, the name corresponds to a number of their 99 names, in particular *al-Qayyum* and *al-Malik*.

[18] Exod. 15:20-21.

[19] Luke 1:45-53.

[20] My chapter on Psalm 91 offers suggestions along this line.

[21] *The Bay Psalm Book* was published in 1640, just 20 years after the Mayflower landed at Plymouth Rock.

[22] *The Psalms* (New York: Riverhead, 1997) p. ix.

1: The Choice

[1] Verses 1-3.

[2] Verses 4-5.

[3] Calling Psalms 1 and 2 psalms of orientation, Walter Brueggemann divides all 150 psalms into three categories: orientation, disorientation — where life is messed up — and reorientation; *The Message of the Psalms* (Minneapolis: Fortress, 1985).

2: Coronation Song

[1] The alternative would be to make the psalmist refer hyperbolically to David, Solomon or some other king in his royal line (verses 8-9). No one suggests that David or anyone else in his dynasty extended his rule to the ends of the earth. Even Solomon's rule never extended beyond the Middle East.

"Anointed," the Hebrew word *messiah*, was in an ordinary sense used of every Israelite king (verse 2). So if we were to take the psalm to speak hyperbolically of one of David's imperfect descendants, the background story could have been Absalom's treasonous bid for David's throne or the moment Adonijah and his co-conspirators learned that David had crowned Solomon king instead (2 Sam. 15-19 and 1 Kings 1). Other stories may suggest themselves also because psalms always speak to the human condition, not just isolated incidents in Israelite history.

While a hyperbolic reading of it is possible, the Messianic reading of consensus is far more natural — that far from being replete with deliberate exaggeration, this psalm is to be fulfilled literally in the Messiah, David's greater son. To take it in this way in no way forbids our applying it in part to David's lesser sons.

[2] 1 Chron. 17:11-14 (cf. 2 Sam. 7:16).

[3] Or compilers, plural.

[4] Verses 7-9.

[5] Verse 8. Believing Jesus was the Messiah, his apostles were convinced this spoke of his person, as well as his death and resurrection to reign over the earth (e.g. Acts 13:33). But we can leave the question of ultimate meaning here since it takes us far beyond the psalm itself.

[6] Verse 12.

[7] Muslim readers bothered by this concept need to know it simply refers to the fact that, like God, we think, speak, love, forgive, get angry, etc. That, however, doesn't change the fact that God is infinitely greater, wiser, more powerful, etc., than we are. To say that he loves or gets angry, for example, cannot mean that his love and anger are exactly like ours since he is on another plane of existence entirely.

[8] 1 Kings 21:1-16.

3: Nothing Else Matters

[1] 2 Sam. 13:1-14:24.

[2] 1 Sam. 18:6-9.

[3] 2 Sam. 14:25-15:6.

[4] Verse 2.

[5] As comforting as this concept of God's being on our side is, it's problematic also. For a look at how it works biblically, see my chapter on Psalm 110.

[6] 2 Sam. 18-19.

6: Cry in the Dark

[1] See Psa. 79, 80 and 89, for example.

[2] See also Deut. 28:49-50 (cf. verses 47-48).

[3] This is the whole point of God's reply in Job 38-41. He never answers Job's complaint that he's been unjustly punished. He simply says, "Job, you're way over your head, trying to sort these things out. Leave them to me."
For the broader context of God's reply to Job, see my chapter on Psalm 7.

[4] We see reciprocity in many biblical passages—for example, Gen. 2:17, Deut. 30:15-20, 2 Chron. 26:5b, 16 and Prov. 3:33-35. But already in Genesis, right alongside reciprocity, we find reversal again and again too. Cain's murder of the righteous Abel (chapter 4) and Joseph's mistreatment at the hands of both his brothers and his master Potiphar (chapters 37 and 39) show us people suffering unjustly. On the other hand, we see sinners blessed when they cry out to God like Jacob did in chapter 32 and sometimes simply because of God's mercy to them—for example, Adam and Eve (chapter 3), Abraham (chapter 20) and Joseph's brothers (chapters 43-45). We see this same reversal right through the Tanakh and on into the New Testament.

[5] Reversal undergirds the Torah's entire law code, but we see it most plainly in the cultic requirements of sacrifice for sin and the related purification rituals. Without the atonement they signify, there could be no covenant between God and humankind.

7: God of Justice, God of Truth

[1] Verse 4.

[2] Genesis 2:17 warns that death would be the immediate outcome of their disobedience and while it clearly began its sinister work in both Eve and Adam the instant they sinned, they lived on for many years afterwards.

[3] Whether corporate or personal, many of the injustices we face cry out at the very least for an explanation as to why God doesn't intervene. So much so that many have turned away from God rather than endure in the face of horrendous evil what Helmut Thielicke termed "the silence of God." For more on this see his *The Silence of God* translated with an introduction by Geoffrey W. Bromiley (Grand Rapids: Eerdmans, 1962).

I have no trouble understanding those who have so abandoned God. But I can't think how their doing so does them any good except in the way that it does a man with a migraine good to smash his head against a wall. We're far wiser to accept God's silence—let God be God—and do what the psalmist does here. Namely, pour out his heart to him in all his pain, confusion and fiery indignation.

8: Such Wisdom, Such Wildness

[1] Verses 5-8 refer to Genesis 1:28-30. This act of committing the earth to our care is all about God's making us responsible as stewards under him. It has nothing to do with his licensing us to abuse the earth in God's good name. For more on this, see chapter 24b, "The Earth Is the Lord's."

[2] Being created in God's likeness, we are finite embodiments of what our Creator is infinitely (Gen. 1:26-30). God isn't *anthropomorphic*—doesn't possess human attributes. Rather, we are *theomorphic*—physical representations of the invisible God. Our mouths speak as God does without a physical mouth, our hands create as he does without physical hands, etc. While he's on another level of being entirely, we are genuinely like him. We aren't animal only. Like him, we are spiritual and moral beings and we are in direct relationship with him.

To any Muslim readers afraid that this approaches idolatry, I would argue that regardless of how uncomfortable we are with it, all divine-human relationship—whether positive or negative, whether we elicit God's pleasure or incur his anger—involves belief in divine-human likeness. All verbal revelation of God, likewise, presupposes divine-human likeness in order for us to understand it.

9: God of Impossibility

[1] For a discussion of the issue of God's being on our side, see my chapter on Psalm 110.

[2] Verse 13.

[3] Verses 19-20.
[4] Verses 9-11.
[5] Otherwise their blood wouldn't need to be avenged (verse 12).
[6] Gen.3:4-5.

10: Who Are the Poor?

[1] We may say only "This is what poor people do" but our point is implicitly that all poor people do it.

[2] One thing that does skew the ratio of good to bad budgeters among the poor is alcoholism and drug addiction, which effectively make budgeting impossible.

[3] The inequities that exist between G8 countries and countries in the Developing World are undeniably gross and demand swift justice. But we must never use the urgency of that issue to justify our disregard for the needy on our very doorsteps.

[4] The prophets reserve some of their most scathing attacks for arrogant religious people. Amos, for example, says God abhors Israel's arrogance (Amos 6:8) and Jeremiah that God will judge Israel for its overweening pride (Jer. 49:16; cf. Zeph. 3:11-12).

[5] Eugene Peterson speaks of this in his *Answering God: The Psalms as Tools for Prayer* (San Francisco: HarperCollins, 1989) pp. 98-99.

[6] Verses 2, 12-14, 17-18.

[7] Verses 12-15.

[8] Anyone who has experienced poverty knows that the poor sometimes prey on the poor too. Again what's important isn't class so much as the choice to live as if God doesn't care if we take advantage of the vulnerable.

[9] Prov. 6:6-11, 20:4, 21:25.

[10] Prov. 14:31, 19:17, 21:13.

[11] On our having been created in God's likeness, see note 2 in chapter 8 above.

14: Of Scoundrels and Fools

[1] Verse 1.

[2] I would remind any Muslim readers appalled at the thought that believers too are guilty of practical atheism, of the repeated Quranic emphasis on how frequently we all—even believers—forget God. See for example, 20:115 which shows the Prophet Adam forgetting God.

[3] Genesis 25-32 tells the unsavory Jacob's story until his stupendous wrestling match with God.

15: The Trouble With Goodness

[1] Andy Wachowski (director), *The Matrix* (Los Angeles: Warner Brother, 1999).

[2] Psalm 27:4, 61:4 and 84:2-4 voice the psalmist's desire to live in God's house or tent, which can be taken figuratively as referring to living in oneness with the God who shelters us from all harm.

19: The Fear That Frees

[1] *The Idea of the Holy* (London: Oxford University Press, 1924).
[2] Gen. 3:10, Exod. 20:18-21 and Psa. 19:7-11.
[3] Genesis 4.

22: For the Abandoned of the Earth

[1] In Steinbeck's *The Grapes of Wrath* (New York: Penguin, 2006) and Cuppola's *Apocalypse Now* (San Francisco: Zoetrope Studios, 1979).
[2] *Holy the Firm* (New York: Harper & Row, 1984) p. 49.
[3] Verse 15.
[4] He famously uttered the psalmist's opening cry of abandonment on the cross (Matt. 27:46, Mark 15:34).
[5] Verse 24.
[6] Verse 31.

23: Shepherd Song

[1] Matt. 6:34.
[2] Verses 1-3.
[3] Verse 5.

24a: Freedom in the Face of Fear

[1] Lest anyone accuse the writers of the Tanakh implicit adherence to polytheism (e.g. in Psalm 29:1) we need to see that they simply acknowledged the existence of a multiplicity of spiritual beings opposed to God. They were at great pains to present the gods as decidedly inferior to him and in no sense deserving of anyone's worship. On this point the Jewish, Christian and Muslim scriptures are in complete agreement.
[2] See Gen. 25-33.
[3] By *empty* I mean simply that no idol was seated on it. This would have been the most stunning thing about it in the ancient world. To the idolatrous peoples surrounding Israel, this was precisely the place to put your idol. To carry an empty throne around made a real statement about the holy, transcendent God you served.
[4] 2 Sam. 6.

24b: The Earth is the Lord's

[1] I refer to Stephen Harper's Conservative government.

[2] How many more Gulf spills must earth endure before we realize our petroleum-dependent way of life has to end?

[3] Quoted by Thomas L. Friedman in *Hot, Flat, and Crowded* (New York: Farrar, Straus & Giroux, 2008) p. 49.

[4] While the rate of tropical rainforest clear-cutting has fallen off somewhat over the past couple of years, it was previously as high as one acre per second.

[5] If this lifestyle wasn't clearly documented as insane before 2000 CE, everything since then points to that. But already a decade on, many of us continue to live in a bubble of unreality, willingly ignorant of the juggernaut of global population growth and consumption of earth's nonrenewable resources. For an introduction to those realities—our degradation of earth's biosphere and our reduction of earth's biodiversity—see Friedman's *Hot, Flat, and Crowded.*

[6] There are now sufficient scientific data to establish that earth can no longer sustain its growing population and to insist that we not only alter our use of earth's limited resources radically, but do all we can to achieve zero population growth too.

When my wife and I had our kids, we saw no connection between family size in sparsely populated Canada and earth's limited resources. But we added not just four more mouths to feed, but four more Canadians to indulge themselves as our culture virtually requires us to do. The issue may be less overpopulation than the over-indulgence of our culture. On average, four Bangladeshis use a mere fraction of the resources four North Americans use annually and our over-consumption is tragically mirrored in our waste output too. Our greatly heightened awareness of real cost to the environment—resources taken, pollution added—means that we, even more than Bangladeshis, need to commit to limiting our population growth.

[7] But it's not just about Western selfishness. Another part of the problem is that we've taken so many things for granted for so long, without really considering sustainability or having accurate means of measuring our impact on it. My high school social studies teacher very seriously warned that within a decade there'd be standing room only on planet earth. That was back in the 70's! Only in the last 10-20 years have our measurements and tracking developed sufficiently to make accurate predictions about the future of our planet. Now with each passing year the problem of earth's dwindling resources becomes clearer. Our rampant consumerism and earth's fast-growing population are by anyone's reckoning a deadly combination.

[8] Gen. 1:28-30. As Frederick Buechner says, "The holy earth. We must take such care of it. It must take such care of us. This side of Paradise, we are each of us so nearly all the other has." *Whistling in the Dark: An ABC Theologized* (San Francisco: Harper & Row, 1988) p. 40.

[9] Gen. 1:28.

[10] *Mother Country: Britain, the Welfare State and Nuclear Pollution* (New York: Farrar, Straus & Giroux, 1989) p. 30.

[11] See chapter 24a for the significance of chaos in this psalm.

[12] Verses 3-6.

25: The Secret of Life

[1] Verses 2-3,15-20.
[2] Verses 4-5, 8-10, 12.
[3] Verse 15.
[4] Lone Scherfig (director), *An Education* (Los Angeles: BBC Films, 2009).
[5] Gen. 18.
[6] Lev. 11:44-45, 19:2, 20:8, 20:26, 21:8, 21:23, 22:9.
[7] Verses 21, 8.
[8] Verses 4-5.
[9] Verses 9, 12.
[10] Verse 11.
[11] Some of our religious leaders are undeniably shallow, dishonest and greedy. But despicable as their treachery is, reducing all religion to sleaze and underhandedness is far too easy to be true. We mustn't turn the exception into the rule simply because in our media bad news sells far more than good.
[12] Verses 5, 15, 21.

27: In the Eye of the Storm

[1] Quoted by Candace Bushnell in "Rake's Progress," *Vogue* (July 1995) p. 174.
[2] Verse 8.
[3] Verses 7-9 and 11-12.
[4] Verses 1-3, 5-6 and 10.
[5] *In the First Circle*, translated by Harry T. Willetts (New York: Harper Perennial, 2009) p. 95.

29: God of All Truth

[1] See his *The Meaning and End of Religion* (Minneapolis: Fortress Press, 1991).
[2] We don't help anyone by becoming all things to all people, which is an impossible feat, after all. Rather we're most helpful to others when we're being most fully ourselves.

32: Amazing Grace

[1] *The Dark Night of the Soul: A Psychiatrist Explores the Connection Between Darkness and Spiritual Growth* (New York: HarperCollins, 2004) p. 55.
[2] *Ibid.*, 59.

[3] Verse 3. For a very readable treatment of this topic, see Dr. Gabor Maté's thought provoking book, *When the Body Says No: The Cost of Hidden Stress* (Toronto: Vintage Canada) 2004.

[4] Knowing the *Truth of God's Love: The One Thing We Can't Live Without* (Ann Arbor: Servant Books, 1988) p. 27.

[5] Quoted by Kreeft, *ibid.*

42/43: Thirst

[1] Psalm 43:3-4.

[2] For more help on the topic of depression, see Michael D. Yapko's *Breaking Patterns of Depression* (1997) and Daniel G. Amen's *Change Your Brain, Change Your Life: (*1999).

46: A Tale of Two Cities

[1] Verses. 8-9.

[2] Gen. 32:24-31.

[3] Exod. 14:27.

[4] 2 Kings 18:17-19:37.

[5] (New York: Houghton Mifflin, 2002). This quotation comes not from the book, but from a 1964 CBS documentary called "The Silent Spring of Rachel Carson."

[6] "Call It Democracy," *World of Wonders* (Burlington: True North Records, 1995).

[7] Even though the army she refers to was totally annihilated.

51: Sinners Made New

[1] Walt Kelly, 1971.

[2] For more on this topic, see my chapter on Psalm 14.
Tradition credits King David with writing Psalm 51 after he'd committed adultery and murdered his lover's husband. Some Muslims will react to this since the Qur'an never details the sins of the prophet David. In fact, despite their routinely praying for the Prophet Muhammad's salvation, Muslims have traditionally been uncomfortable with the very idea of prophets who sin. They are especially disturbed to learn that the Tanakh details such heinous sins as this, making David as unsavory a character as he is exemplary in other respects. There is great hope for us in this, though, as it tells us that no sin is too great for the mercy and grace of our God to cover it.

62: Life on the Edge

[1] HIV infection rates have decreased significantly due to DTES safe injection sites.

[2] I don't mean to suggest that the way we dealt with mental health patients in the 1980's didn't call for a major overhauling because it unquestionably did. But pulling the plug on everything was far too easy a solution to so complex a problem for it to take proper care of their needs.

[3] For a glimpse of the human face of Africa's AIDS crisis, see Stephanie Nolen's book *28: Stories of AIDS in Africa* (New York: Walker & Company, 2007).

[4] See Rebecca Clarren's hard-hitting article "Paradise Lost: Greed, Sex Slavery, Forced Abortions and Right-Wing Moralists" at http://www.msmagazine.com/spring2006/paradise_full.asp

[5] Verses 3-4, 10. On our creation in God's likeness, see note 2 in chapter 8 above.

[6] Verse 10.

[7] Verse 4b.

[8] Verses 11-12.

[9] Verses 1-2, 5-8.

65: Between Friends

[1] The psalmist gives us two pictures of this friendship: living our lives in God's presence and being fully at home in his home—i.e. the temple in Jerusalem (verse 4). Muslims may struggle with this idea, fearing it implies equality with God. But the Bible never sees it as lessening God's greatness or suggesting that he has any peers. Having said that, though, real communion with God, the closeness of friends, is modeled by one psalmist after another. It is also why Abraham is called the friend of God (2 Chron. 20:7; cf. Qur'an 4:124).

[2] See my chapter on Psalm 14.

[3] See my chapter on Psalm 126.

[4] Along with free choice in nearly all things spiritual, New Age spirituality grants us the right to do what we want morally. And for most people, that's what gives it such appeal: you answer only to yourself for your moral choices.

[5] See my chapter on Psalm 76.

[6] Verse 3.

[7] Verse 4.

[8] Verses 5-7.

[9] As Eugene Peterson says in *Leap Over A Wall*, "We're most human when we deal with God. Any other way of life leaves us less human, less ourselves" (New York: HarperCollins, 1997) p. 75.

[10] *Why Religion Matters: The Fate of the Human Spirit in an Age of Disbelief* (San Francisco: HarperCollins, 2001) p. 231.

[11] Verses 9-13.

76: Perfect Hero

[1] Verse 10.

[2] See my chapter on Psalm 10 for more on this.

[3] In fairness, nihilists see biblical faith as escapism too, as our projecting ourselves onto the screen of the universe in the overblown form of God. And likewise Buddhists see it as merely further elaboration of an illusory world. But the fact remains that we don't get to choose the nature of reality. We either accept it or seek to escape it.

87: City of God

[1] Dallas Willard wryly observes of the world's great religions that: "If [their] founders had spoken as [their followers] do today, the corresponding religions simply would not be here"; *Knowing Christ Today: Why We Can Trust Spiritual Knowledge* (San Francisco: HarperCollins, 2009) p. 9.

By "every serious religious teacher," I in no wise mean to belittle religious pluralists, who are just as serious about promoting their pluralism as Eckhart Tolle, for example, is about promoting his ideas; e.g. see his *The Power of Now: A Guide to Spiritual Enlightenment* (Novato: New World Library, 1999). Pluralists undeniably present their framework as the nature of reality — unflinching fact. But by putting all things religious inside it, they relegate all the different versions of truth to the realm of personal opinion, no one version being any truer than another. We can only say what's truer for (i.e. more useful to) you or me personally.

On the one hand, religious pluralists can be very passionate about religion. For example, see Huston Smith's thought provoking *Why Religion Matters* (2001). But on the other hand, what they promote is religion-as-pluralism. Making all religions equally true within their larger framework of religious oneness, they encourage religious sampling, letting adherents decide the importance of the various religious choices offered largely by their own interest or lack of interest in them.

[2] *A Faith for This One World?* (London: SCM Press, 1961) p. 30.

[3] *Knowing Christ* (2009) p. 3; original in italics.

[4] *Ibid.*, p. 7.

[5] Gen. 12:3.

[6] Verse 1.

[7] Psa. 86:9.

[8] Isa. 18.

[9] Verse 4.

[10] Verses 4-6, i.e. in the Hebrew text.

[11] Verse 6.

[12] Verse 7.

[13] Isa. 2:14.

90: On the Meaning of Life

[1] Clive James, "Better Than Reality," Nov. 6, 2009. http://news.bbc.co.uk/2/hi/

uk_news/magazine/8347259.stm

[2] *Ibid.*

[3] Verses 1-2.

[4] The psalmist has in mind here suffering resulting from the sins of his people. Otherwise he wouldn't be asking God to replace their affliction with joy (verses 13-15).

[5] Verse 12.

[6] See Martin Heidegger's *Being and Time* (Albany: State University of New York Press, 1996).

91: The Poetry of Faith

[1] Verses 1-5.

[2] Verses 3, 6, 13.

[3] Verses 7-8.

[4] Verse 15.

[5] Verses 1, 14.

[6] *Cornerstone Biblical Commentary, vol. 7* (Carol Stream: Tyndale House, 2009) pp. 297-98.

[7] Dan. 6.

[8] Based on a quotation from Brian Gerrish given by Mark D. Futato in *Interpreting the Psalms* (2007) p. 42.

103: Awesome God

[1] Verses 8-12.

[2] Verses 6-7.

[3] Lev. 17:11.

[4] Verses 17-18.

[5] Verse 19.

110: God on Our Side

[1] If the invasion of Iraq under President George Bush Sr. was not uncalled for—a point many would debate—the second invasion under President George Bush Jr. certainly was.

[2] Psalm 1:2.

[3] Verse 1.

[4] So the picture is of God's leading a military campaign alongside his appointed king.

[5] Verse 4.

[6] Genesis 14:17-20. It's significant that Melchizedek was "king of Salem,"

meaning "peace" (verse 18) and tradition identifies Salem as the pre-Davidic Jerusalem. We often say, "There's no lasting peace without justice." Melchizedek would have surely agreed.

[7] Verses 1-3.

[8] Verses 5-7.

[9] Implicit here is the idea that his conquest is unhindered by exhaustion. With just a drink and no time for a rest, Yahveh and his anointed king carry their triumph to the ends of the earth.

[10] *God's Politics: Why the Right Gets It Wrong and the Left Doesn't Get It* (New York: HarperCollis, 2005) p. xviii. So it is here: the king conquers only because he fights alongside Yahveh to ensure that *his* will for his world be obeyed.

120: In the Desperate Pause Between Wars

[1] My title was inspired by David R. Slavitt's translation of verse 7 in *Sixty-one Psalms of David* (New York: Oxford University Press, 1996) p. 100.

I don't mean to minimize the fact that America, Canada and the rest of NATO are presently at war. But having said that, we'd do well to remember that a far more devastating war than anything fought on the far side of the world may yet issue from our largely *carte blanc* approach to Israel. The reality is that it could yet push us into either a full-on terrorist war on home turf or a nuclear war in the Middle East on the scale of the Holocaust.

[2] How many who call themselves Christians can list all of the Ten Commandments and all twelve apostles—or was it Twelve Commandments and ten apostles? How many of us can recite the Apostle's Creed or speak intelligently about the Sermon on the Mount, assuming we know what it is?

My point isn't to belittle the majority of Christians. It's just to say that there's a huge range of understanding—to say nothing of misunderstanding—that goes by the name of Christian. Like everyone else, Christians wax and wane in their personal devotion, depending on what we had for breakfast and a whole lot of other things. Which is why our actions so often belie our faith professions. Again, my point isn't to lament so much as to simply acknowledge the fact that attempting to cover all that diversity with a single word is bound to distort.

[3] I don't mean to dispute the fact that most Christians, Muslims and Jews, etc., hold many beliefs in common with others of their particular faith. My objection is only to reification, turning abstract concepts into concrete (albeit imaginary) objects. And nearly always doing so surreptitiously, unconsciously.

This linguistic sloppiness breeds many problems. To begin, it's dishonest. For example, saying "Christianity teaches…" is different from saying "The Catholic Church teaches…" The latter exists as a concrete entity, with physical headquarters in Rome, etc. So we'd most likely be referring to official Vatican teaching, which again is concrete. But the abstraction "Christianity" is not like an actual church or denomination. Yet we use it as if it was, usually smuggling in our particular understanding or ideal version of Christian faith in the process. So we typically say "Christianity teaches the importance of the sacraments" when *our* denomination does so.

The biggest problem with this is the false authority it confers. Essentially, we pretend to speak either for the sum total of all Christians or for the ideal—that is, for true Christianity. While the former is impossible, the latter—without a direct line to heaven—is ludicrous.

Adherents of non-Christian religions are often guilty of this same sleight-of-hand. Moderate Akhbar Ahmed and extremist Anwar al-Alaki both champion what "Islam" teaches. But ironically each presents a vision diametrically opposed to that of the other, which is actually just his particular take on Islam. Of course, neither one is making things up. The fact is, the Qur'an can be read both ways.

When it comes to reifying religions other than our own, we're on thinner ice still. What gives me, a Christian, the right to say which version of Islam is the true one? If we're honest here, we're just promoting the version that best suits *our* purposes.

Please note that I'm not arguing for more "objectivity" in our treatment of Muslim faith and practice. As Thomas Kuhn demonstrated in *The Structure of Scientific Revolutions* (Chicago: University of Chicago Press, 1996) all our objectivity is a myth. And what's true of scientific discourse is equally true of religious discourse. We all tell it slant—there's no escaping that.

What I am urging is that we non-Muslims be honest about which particular stream of the Muslim faith we're presenting. We need also to be truthful and fair in speaking of those Muslims we disagree with—speaking our minds without apology and yet acknowledging that even our opponents may offer helpful correctives.

For a much fuller discussion of the dangers of reification, see Wilfred Cantwell Smith's *The Meaning and End of Religion* (Minneapolis: Fortress Press, 1991).

[4] Gingrich's "stealth jihad" probably comes from that master of verbal assault, Daniel Pipes, who spoke of "stealth Islamists" back in 2004. Sadly, both men fit Maya Angelou's description of "...mouths spilling words/Armed for slaughter"; from her poem "On the Pulse of Morning," *The Complete Collected Poems of Maya Angelou* (New York: Random House, 1994) p. 270.
http://www.aei.org/docLib/Address%20by%20Newt%20Gingrich07292010.pdf
http://www.danielpipes.org/1841/stealth-islamist-khaled-abou-el-fadl

[5] http://www.bbc.co.uk/news/world-us-canada-11434953

[6] *Ibid.*

[7] Psalm 35:20.

[8] To judge American Muslims by Shariah law on this point would be akin to granting fundamentalist Mormon elders the right to marry multiple underage brides on the basis of their religious beliefs.

[9] But mustn't we be vigilant lest we lose our hard-won rights and freedoms to regressive laws? Absolutely. And none more so than the rights and freedoms of women. But having said that, we mustn't give in to paranoia over Muslim attempts to gain court acceptance of Shariah law either. On the one hand, we can hardly fault our Shariah-keeping Muslims for trying. But on the other hand, our judges must

not be asleep at the switch. And we in turn must be assiduously on guard to ensure that any court rulings contradicting our societal values are overturned.

On the vital importance of vigilance against anything threatening America's liberty for all, see David Dark's excellent book *The Gospel According to America: A Meditation on a God-blessed, Christ-haunted Idea* (Louisville: Westminster John Knox Press, 2005). I am fully aware of the threat posed to American ideals by radical Islamists. But to be truly effective, says Dark, that vigilance must include the saving power of self-doubt (pp. 9-12). On the same theme, Michael Ignatieff in *The Lesser Evil: Political Ethics in an Age of Terror* (Princeton: Princeton University Press, 2005) writes of the importance of protecting democracy not just from its enemies, but *from ourselves also* (see chapter 1). To do that effectively requires a measure of self-doubt totally forbidden by today's media pundits.

[10] http://www.aei.org/docLib/Address%20by%20Newt%20Gingrich07292010.pdf For more on this, see note 3 above.

[11] This approach focuses on all of the Qur'an's most tolerant passages, for example, ignoring its numerous militant passages.

[12] Gingrich's "stealth jihad" leaves us fearing that all Muslims—especially those who most deny it—secretly want to impose Shariah law on America.

[13] The effects of this distortion are profound. America's moderate Muslim youth are increasingly vulnerable to extremist preachers like American-born Anwar al-Awlaki in our heightened post-9-11 sensitivity. And they owe their vulnerability to a variety things. First to their sense of simultaneously being always in the spotlight in America since 9-11 and yet feeling isolated from their fellow-Americans due to what moderates call their "identity theft" by radicals like Osama bin Laden. Equally disturbing is this very distortion I speak of, which asks our Muslim youth to choose between half-truths, and the fear of Islam which underlies it. Then too they're influenced by a Western youth culture which encourages rebellion and revolution but wastes it mainly on self-centeredness and decadence.

Another major factor is the obvious disconnect between the America which champions democracy all over the world and the America which financially underwrites Israel's trashing of democratic values vis-a-vis its 3.8 million—mainly Muslim—Palestinians (US Census Bureau 2006 figure, inclusive of the Gaza strip). And last but not least, 9-11 helped us see the myth of our invulnerability for what it is. Though very different in kind, the combined attacks of Islamists and the Chinese could one day bring about America's fall, just as the marauding Visagoths and Vandals brought down mighty Rome. Unless we grant justice to the Palestinians, that is.

All these things make America's Muslim youth vulnerable to radical voices. And the fact that their vulnerability is matched by a well-funded extremist recruiting campaign, with now over 4500 websites—up from 6 in 1998—makes the urgency of this problem inescapable.

On Muslim isolation, see:
http://www.bbc.co.uk/news/world-us-canada-11381941 and
http://www.bbc.co.uk/news/world-us-canada-11434953
On the growth of recruiting websites, see:

http://www.washingtonpost.com/wp-dyn/content/article/2010/09/21/
AR2010092101208.html

[14] www.bbc.co.uk/news/world-us-canada-11076846

[15] On the inseparability of liberty and vigilance so vital to American democracy
see David Dark's *Gospel According to America* (2005) pp. 9-12.

126: The Law of Attraction

[1] (New York: Atria Books, 2006) p. 83. Byrne's book was a follow-up on her
movie by the same name. Combined earnings from her movie and book have
reputedly netted Byrne well over $300 million. And her second book, *The Power*
(2010) promises her more of the same success.

[2] Seeing everything through the law of attraction, as through a lens, its
proponents find proofs for their—or other people's—success in harnessing its power,
whether positively or negatively. Event A is seen as a case of attracting good things
and event B of failing to do so. But it's not alway as clear as it may seem: being
laid off can be viewed both positively and negatively if, say, you're leaving a toxic
workplace and yet will miss your much-needed income. How to decide which way
to read it? Since prosperity consciousness is all about you, it follows that you alone
make all those calls, which in turn increases your sense of power.

But no matter how convinced you are, you can't help but see through this lens
selectively. Because there's no way every single thought you have is a precursor
of reality. And how many times you have to think something for it to happen is
anybody's guess.

So the law of attraction is nowhere near as helpful as it first seems. All it really
does is give people some sense of control in a world where their lives are shaped
by forces far bigger than they and often seem to be threatened by chaos. That is, a
sense of control apart from real prayer to and real faith in God, who is unfailingly in
control.

The hidden danger in the apparently user-friendly law of attraction, though, is
that it strongly tends towards obsessive-compulsiveness. Because the more I want
something, the more I'm going to have to believe it into existence. And the more
unlikely it is, humanly speaking, the more obsessively I'm going to have to hold onto
it mentally, despite all indications to the contrary. So I can easily become both out
of touch with reality and psychotic (i.e. obsessive-compulsive) in a sincere effort to
better my life.

[3] Verses 5-6.

130: The Love That Will Not Let Me Go

[1] *Book of Longing* (Toronto: McClelland & Stewart, 2006) p. 159.

[2] Verse 4.

[3] Dietrich Bonhoeffer coined the term "cheap grace" in *The Cost of Discipleship*

translated by R.H. Fuller with some revision by Irmgard Booth (London: SCM Press, 2001).

[4] Peter Kreeft writes of this in *Truth of God's Love*, pp. 26-30.

[5] Verse 8.

131: In God's Arms

[1] *Third-Class Superhero* (New York: Harcourt, 2006) p. 28.

[2] "New Rules in American Life: Searching for Self-fullfillment in a World Turned Upside Down," *Psychology Today* (April 1981) p. 50.

[3] 1 Sam. 17.

[4] This concept of submission is very much like the Quranic (i.e. pre-Sufi Muslim) understanding. It never involves the denial of personality. It denies only personality's distortion, abuse and misuse.

[5] "Little Gidding" in *Four Quartets* (London: Faber & Faber, 1959) p. 59. Original in parenthesis.

133: Peace Train, Holy Roller

[1] (New York: Riverhead, 2005).

[2] Exod. 30:22-25, Lev. 8:1-12.

[3] Jeremy Brown, http://www.bbc.co.uk/news/world-middle-east-10656890

137: The Jagged Edge of Justice

[1] While C.S. Lewis didn't deal specifically with Psalm 137, he failed to see the value of any of the psalmists' prayers for vengeance, calling them all morally "contemptible." *Reflections on the Psalms* (New York: Harcourt, 1958) pp. 21-22. Yet we all feel these same emotions at times, emotions that destroy families and friendships and have the power to destroy us too, unless we first give them to God.

[2] Verses 8-9. I render it simply "blessed."

One of the great things about a word like *'esher* is that there's a whole range of meaning possible for us as readers, depending on how dark and bleak our outlook is. While the word's basic meaning is "blessed," one person can read it as "lucky" and another as "God-sanctioned" without doing the text any injustice. The point being that God wants to free us to tell him how we're actually feeling. Because it's only in such brutal honesty that we give our darkest thoughts and feelings to him and in so doing are mysteriously set free from them.

[3] Verses 5-6.

[4] See my chapter on Psalm 76.

139: The Anatomy of Hate

[1] Pelikan, Jaroslav (ed.), *Sacred Writings [vol. 1]: Judaism: The Tanakh* (New York: Jewish Publication Society, Quality Paperback Book Club, 1992) p. 1274. Robert Alter's *The Book of Psalms: A Translation with Commentary* renders it "Who say your name to scheme…" (New York: W.W. Norton, 2007) p. 483. And John Goldingay describes these men as "the sort of people who live religiously upright lives and are well respected in the community, when they speak of Yhwh or take up Yhwh's name, they do so 'in connection with emptiness'" Tremper Longman III (ed.), *Baker Commentary on the Old Testament Wisdom and Psalms, Psalms: Vol. 3: Psalms 90-150* (Grand Rapids: Baker, 2008) p. 637. So they use God's name deceptively and their falsehood and violence combine to make them God's enemies.

[2] The wording here is the very same as in the Ten Commandments (Exod. 20:7). Their use of God's name is futile because it in no wise does what it claims to do—that is, divinely sanction their evil deeds. It is also futile in the sense that God will ultimately overthrow all they build.

[3] Ironically, many who totally reject hatred themselves hate Westboro's pastor, often without knowing it.

[4] *Shawshank Redemption* (Beverly Hills: Castle Rock Entertainment, 1994).

[5] *The Matrix* (1999).

[6] Matt. 5:22, 44.

Those commentators on Psalm 139 who point out that "totally reject" or "refuse to tolerate" are perfectly legitimate lexical entries for *hate* in Hebrew are absolutely correct. But I'm reluctant to approach the text as they do for the simple reason that we function as wholes, not isolated parts. None of us can hermetically seal off whatever strong moral positions we take from the realm of our emotions. To "totally reject" an evildoer is to feel the emotion that goes with total rejection—what we'd normally call *hatred*. There's no wrong either in rejecting such evildoers or in feeling very strongly about it. Indeed, both are good and right provided we cathartically give all such hatred to God as the psalmist does here. It's only in not doing so—in nursing and managing our hatred on our own—that we sin and succumb to its destructive power.

[7] St. Augustine said we're to love our enemies, but not God's enemies. I agree, as long as we understand with Augustine that simply disobeying God doesn't make a person his enemy in this sense of the word. Because that would include everyone. Nor do we have the right to single out the sinners we personally find repulsive—say, murderers or adulterers.

No, the psalmist specifically hates only those who embrace injustice and violence in God's name. All sins are not equal in God's eyes. Psalm 11:5 says that God hates those who give themselves to violence—and the Hebrew word here includes the ideas of oppression, cruelty and injustice also.

If God hates such people, how can it be wrong for us to hate them too? Is our goodness somehow to surpass his? Or have we Christians not smoothed out one too

many wrinkles between justice and love?
⁸ Verses 1-12.
⁹ Verses 13-18.
¹⁰ Verses 19-24.

146: The Importance of Praise

¹ (New York: Harcourt, 1986) pp. 93-94.
² *Ibid.*, p. 94.
³ *Ibid.*
⁴ *Ibid.*, pp. 94-95.
⁵ *Ibid.*, pp. 96-97.
⁶ For a true, albeit fictional, account of one woman's reasons for becoming homeless, see Marilynne Robinson's haunting novel *Housekeeping* (New York: Picador, 1980).
⁷ *The Psalms*, p. x.

150: Unending Song

¹ Professor Charles J. Adams related this anecdote in a class on the Islamic Tradition in McGill University's Institute of Islamic Studies, January 1984. Neither the Qur'an nor the Hadiths have anything good to say about music. Hence the near illegality of all music in Islamist regimes. Moderate Muslims rarely hold to such austerity. But with the sole exception of the Sufis, Muslims do not permit the use of music in the worship of God at all.
² *The Language and Imagery of the Bible* (Philadelphia: Westminster Press, 1980) p. 28.
³ 2 Sam. 6:14-22.
⁴ *The Death of Adam* (New York: Picador, 2005) pp. 238-39.
⁵ *Interaction of Color*, Revised ed. (New Haven: Yale University Press, 1975) p. 2.

Acknowledgments

I am deeply grateful to Miriam Thomas and Raymond Leung for reading and commenting on my manuscript in its entirety. Also to Joyce Rees, Helen Auperlee, Sharon Milligan, Simon Patey and members of the Jacob's Well Thursday team for reading and commenting on it in part, along with my good friends Stephen Millier and Marg Yeo. While their generous help and advice have doubtless improved it greatly, I alone am responsible for whatever errors remain. I am grateful to Wendy Muth for her invaluable editorial help and also to librarians Bill Badke and Abraham Brake for their kind assistance.

In the absence of a bibliography, I want to express my debt of gratitude to the many biblical scholars whose work has shaped and informed my understandings here. They include:

Raymond Dillard

Robert Alter

Bruce Walke

Dietrich Bonhoeffer

Harvie M. Conn

St. Augustine

Walter Brueggemann

Eugene H. Peterson

Jonathan Magonet

Tremper Longman III

Willem A. VanGemeren

Kevin J. Vanhooser

Marva J. Dawn

Mark Futato

John Goldingay

Peter C. Craigie

N.T. Wright

Gavriel Rubin

James L. Mays

Derek Kidner

Vern S. Poythress

Marvin E. Tate

G.B. Caird

John Calvin

David R. Slavitt
A.A. Anderson
Leslie C. Allen
Nahum M. Sarna
Calvin Seerveld
M.H. Mykoff
Jerome F.D. Creach
Lawrence A. Hoffman
E.S. Gerstenberger
Stephen Mitchell
Erich Zenger

Meredith G. Kline
Leslie S. M'Caw
Artur Weiser
Craig A. Blaising
William G. Braude
J.A. Motyer
Moshe Schapiro
David G. Firth
Carmen S. Hardin
Philip S. Johnston

...and with them, that great host of nameless biblical scribes and translators, both Jewish and Christian, without whose work I could never have done mine.

Permissions

The author and publisher gratefully acknowledge permission to reprint the following previously published materials:

Excerpt from BROTHER TO A DRAGONFLY, copyright © 2000 by Will D. Campell. Printed with permission from the Continuum International Publishing Group

Excerpt from THE MESSAGE: THE BIBLE IN CONTEMPORARY LANGUAGE, Eugene Peterson, 2002. pp. 910-11. Used by permission of NavPress, all rights reserved. www.navpress.com

Excerpt from ON THE PULSE OF MORNING by Maya Angelou, copyright © 1993 by Maya Angelou. Used by permission of Random House, Inc.

Excerpt from "401k" in THIRD CLASS SUPERHERO, copyright © 2003 by Charles Yu, reprinted by permission of Houghton Mifflin Harcourt Publishing Company.

Excerpts from REFLECTIONS ON THE PSALMS, copyright © 1958 by C.S. Lewis, renewed 1986 by Arthur Owen Barfield, reprinted by permission of Houghton Mifflin Harcourt Publishing Company.

Every effort has been made to trace ownership of copyright

materials. In the event of an inadvertent omission or error, please notify the publisher.

While all web pages cited are online at the time of publication, the publisher cannot guarantee their ongoing availability.

For more information on *Faithsongs* or author Mark Anderson, visit   www.faithsongsonline.com

Jacob's Well is a faith-based community that seeks mutually transformative friendships in Vancouver, Canada's Downtown Eastside. For more information, visit   www.jacobswell.ca